Gate of Remembrance

(1918)

Frederick Bligh Bond

ISBN 0-7661-0779-5

THE GATE OF REMEMBRANCE

THE STORY OF THE PSYCHOLOGICAL EXPERIMENT WHICH RESULTED IN THE DISCOVERY OF THE EDGAR CHAPEL AT GLASTONBURY

BY

FREDERICK BLIGH BOND, F.R.I.B.A.

DIRECTOR OF EXCAVATIONS AT GLASTONBURY ABBEY
AUTHOR OF "THE ARCHITECTURAL HANDBOOK OF GLASTONBURY ABBEY"

SECOND EDITION

OXFORD
B. H. BLACKWELL
BROAD STREET
1918

PLATE I.

GLASTONBURY ABBEY.

View from the site of the north transept, looking towards the Quire.

Frontispiece to Part I

PREFACE TO SECOND EDITION

Two problems in the script have engaged the serious attention of critics. The first and simpler of the two is that which is involved in the language and literary form of the messages. This is a curious patchwork of Low Latin, Middle English of mixed periods, and Modern English of varied style and diction. It is a mosaic of multi-coloured fragments cemented together in a strangely random fashion. This anomaly is the more remarkable from the contrast it presents to the sustained and consistent burden of the script itself, which, as though in obedience to some preordained intention and settled plan, seems to proceed to the presentment, line by line, of a completed whole, with absolute patience and indifference to interruptions. Lapse of time seems of no account. After a break of several hours, the thread is resumed at the point where it had been dropped. The unfinished communications about the Loretto Chapel in 1911 are picked up and spontaneously completed five years later. Nevertheless, the queer patchwork of language is again evident.

For this fact, the following explanation is offered. It will easily be conceded that whatever the source or inspiring influence of these messages, the language in which they are conveyed is the *mechanical side* of the matter, the most assuredly conventional element in the process of transmission. But the obvious instruments are the brains of F.B.B. and J.A. The reasoning and reflective faculties are at the time in abeyance or are otherwise engaged,[1] their attention being entirely diverted: but the storehouse of memories and subconscious impressions latent within are being used, and quite independently used, though concurrently in point of time with the normal use of the thinking faculties on a wholly different subject.

Consider for a moment the human brain as the repository of all impressions made on the mind from childhood upwards. Thus viewed, it becomes, as it were, an encyclopedia of all knowledge which the conscious mind has stored, each item recording an idea of a certain quality, in such language as circumstances may at the time have dictated. Suppose then—and it is not difficult to do so—that each of these records is responsive to the impulse of an Idea which is seeking expression, and whose instrument of expression is some sort of sympathetic vibration attuned to the original thought which recorded the particular memory or subject. The sympathetic vibration lays hold of the denser or physical particles of the record, causing them to respond and to emit their own proper voice.

In other words, the language of the script would be simply the product of the reaction of our brain-records to the sympathetic vibration of Idea, from whatever source arising.

Not that such conditions are always necessary or possible. There are, for example, many quite well-authenticated cases of automatic writing in which not only the idea conveyed is outside the consciousness of the writer, but the language itself is entirely unknown to him, or to her, as the case may be. Take, for example, the many recorded cases of automatic writing in languages unknown to the medium, and sometimes requiring special scholarship to appreciate.

[1] In the latest series of sittings, the rule has been for F.B.B. to read aloud to J.A. during the whole course of the writing, from a novel or other entertaining or amusing book, calculated to retain his attention, and the script resulting has proved to have nothing at all in common with the subject-matter of the book, but forms a related series of essays bearing upon the conquest of matter by spirit.

The explanation seems in this case to be that the mind of the medium is plastic to a more direct spiritual influence which can therefore mould its particles and create a new record for itself. This must have been so in the Gift of Tongues at the Pentecost, and later in the history of the Primitive Church.

The second problem noted by critics is a more difficult one. It concerns the intelligent source of the messages. As to this, I have propounded the view of a Greater Memory transcending, and interpenetrating our own. This theory is suggestive rather than explanatory. It does not, and cannot, explain many things which in our present state of knowledge are inexplicable. Neither does it pretend to cover the whole ground. It is, as I say, merely suggestive. Its virtue is that it excludes no other possible agencies, hence leaving room not only for the exercise of transcendental faculty, such as clairvoyance, but for any variety of *primary* impulse, and for any number or degree of directive agencies capable of employing it.

For as we are obliged by our own experience to acknowledge that our own latent memory is revived and brought out in these scripts by some intelligence working apart from our conscious minds ; and to admit that telepathy between two is involved : so we are also bound to allow the possible presence of a further range of telepathic action working through our minds in the production of these messages. And if we are prepared to agree on the one hand that whereas the physical brain dissolves at death and its action ceases, yet, on the other hand, that a more inward and less material brain, the organ and vehicle of the subconscious or intuitive self, still persists and survives entirely the death of the physical body, and if we consider this more inward brain as composed of finer particles, responsive to the far more rapid movements of intuitive thought, then we shall have to allow that the memory-record of any defunct personality, if capable of response *to the same stimulus of spiritual Will and Idea which can actuate our own*, can be drawn upon in like manner by the energising Intelligence, and again, as in our own case, *without evoking the conscious "spirit" or personality proper to it.* This is surely the meaning of Johannes when he says (p. 95):

"Why cling I to that which is not? It is I, and it is not I, butt part of me which dwelleth in the past, and is bound to that which my carnal soul loved and called 'home' these many years. Yet I, Johannes, amm of many partes, and ye better part doeth other things— Laus, laus Deo!—only that part which remembreth clingeth like memory to what it seeth yet."

Thus it seems to me the problem of personality, in the sense of the conscious personal presence of individuals deceased, need not arise at all in connection with these writings. All that it seems vital to assume is the union of the deeper strata of our own latent mind or dream-consciousness with others of a kindred nature and tone, by virtue of their sympathetic and accordant motion in the presence of a greater and all-inclusive spiritual essence, Idea, or Will, omnipresent and all-permeating, waking into activity all dormant memory-records, and directing them into any channel of mind which by previous preparation on the conscious plane has become receptive and retentive of them.

Still small Voices from a distant Time!—thrilling through the void and stirring faint resonances within the deeps of our own being—the great Telepathy, the true Communion of Mind, the gate of the Knowledge, the Gnosis of the apostle, whose key is Mental Sympathy, the key that the lawyers took away, neither entering themselves, nor suffering others to enter.

No discord can mar this communion, since love and understanding are its law. Death cannot touch it: rather is he Keeper of the Gate. Time, as we know it, here counts for naught, for to the deeper dream-consciousness, a day may be as a thousand years, and a period of trance or sleeping as one tick of the clock.

BRISTOL,
May, 1918.

NOTE

By SIR WILLIAM BARRETT, F.R.S.

As some readers of this remarkable book have thought it too incredible to be a record of fact, but rather deemed it a work of imagination, it may be useful to add my testimony to that given in the book as to the genuineness of the whole narrative.

The author has, I am sure, with scrupulous fidelity and care, presented an accurate record of the scripts obtained through the automatic writing of his friend, together with all the archæological knowledge of the ruins of Glastonbury Abbey that was accessible before the excavations were begun. In order to remove any doubt on this point, before further excavations were made, Mr. Bligh Bond has wisely asked representatives of certain societies to examine the later scripts which refer to the Loretto Chapel, note their contents, and see how far the further excavations may or may not verify any of the statements made in the later scripts.

From any point of view the present book is of great interest. To the student of psychology, who ignores any supernormal acquisition of knowledge and yet accepts the good faith of the author, the problem presents many difficulties. Chance coincidence may be suggested, but this does not carry us far. The question therefore arises, where did the veridical or truth-telling information given in some of these scripts come from? As is so often the case in automatic writing a dramatic form

ix

is taken, and messages purport to come from different deceased people. The subconscious or subliminal self of the automatist, doubtless, is the source of much contained in the scripts, and may possibly be responsible for all the insight shown. But in that case we must confer upon the subconsciousness of the automatist faculties hitherto unrecognised by official science. The author has pointed out, on p. 156, some of the powers the subconscious mind must be assumed to possess; to these we may add a possible telepathic transfer of information between the author and the automatist, and also occasionally the faculty of *clairvoyance*, or a transcendental perceptive power; for, according to the investigations of the author, some of the statements made in the script were unknown to any living person, and not found in historical records, prior to their verification in subsequent excavation. We must, however, be on our guard against the too facile use of words such as " telepathy " and " subliminal consciousness " as a cloak to our ignorance. The history of physical science shows how progress has often been retarded by the use of phrases to account for obscure phenomena—words such as " Phlogiston," " Catalysis," etc., which explained nothing, and now are ridiculed, but which were once used by scientific authorities as unquestionable axioms. It is wiser to acknowledge our ignorance and convey our thanks to the author and his friend for the patient and laborious care with which they have furnished valuable material for future psychological explanation. Nor must we omit to recognise the courage shown by Mr. Bligh Bond in the publication of a work which might possibly jeopardise the high reputation he enjoys.

GLASTONBURY

Grey among the meadows, solitary, bare :
Thy walls dismantled, and thy rafters low,
Naked to every wind and chilly air
That steeps the neighbouring marsh, yet standest thou,
Great cloistral monument of other days !
Though marked by all the storms that beat thee through,
A radiant Parable of heavenly ways
That scarce thy lordly builders guess'd or knew !
Vanishing image of great service done,
Smiling to God under the open sky :
Even in thy translation, stone by stone,
Keeping thy spirit-grace and symmetry,
Through ruined clerestory and broken rood
Our chastened souls with tears ascend to God.

A. M. BUCKTON: from *Songs of Joy.*

" *Even so ye, forasmuch as ye are zealous of spiritual gifts, seek that ye may excel to the edifying of the church.*

" *Wherefore let him that speaketh in an unknown tongue pray that he may interpret.*

" *For if I pray in an unknown tongue, my spirit prayeth, but my understanding is unfruitful.*

" *What is it then ?   I will pray with the spirit and I will pray with the understanding also.*"

1 COR. xiv. 12-15.

CONTENTS

xiii

LIST OF ILLUSTRATIONS

THE GATE OF REMEMBRANCE

THE LOST CHAPEL

THE green isle of Glaston, severed as it was from the outer world by its girdle of marsh and mere, was from old time a haunt of peace. Its history as a religious foundation goes back into the mists of antiquity, and is lost in legend and fable. To this quiet retreat, this secluded stronghold of a more ancient faith, the footsteps of the first Christian missioners were guided, and the company of Eastern pilgrims found rest in its green recesses and a well-guarded focus for the great work of evangelising the isle of Britain.

Successive waves of pagan immigration flooded the land, yet never was the lamp of truth extinguished here; and, stranger still, those who came, though of alien race and custom, cherished the older landmarks and sought not to destroy; for the heritage of Glaston was not the heritage of any individual race, but of all—a trust for Christendom.

Within the sacred precincts the dust of many holy men was preserved, and the church enshrined their relics. She grew great through the pious benefactions of kings and nobles whose memory she kept green. Among these the gifts of the great Saxon King, Edgar, " yclept The Peace-

3

able,"[1] were always gratefully remembered. In the great Abbey Church there was a chapel to his honour, well endowed, and, we doubt not, sumptuously furnished. But it was not esteemed sufficient, and in the day of Richard Bere, the last great building Abbot, it was decided that a new and more glorious monument should be erected to his memory. So we learn from Leland, who saw the chapel as it stood, a completed work, but a few years before the dissolution and ruin of the monastery.

Then came, in 1539, the forced surrender, the barbarous execution of the last Abbot, Whiting, the violation of the shrines, and the dispersal of all the treasures of art and learning stored within the Abbey walls. But of the Edgar Chapel nothing more is heard, save that we can infer from a document we quote that it was standing in the days of Elizabeth. Yet it is doubtful whether it can have lasted through half her reign. And perhaps it was one of the first of the buildings to be utterly destroyed, since even its memory had perished and its form and grandeur were alike forgotten. Those who have seen the delicate and beautiful work at St. George's Chapel in Windsor Castle, or that masterpiece of stonecraft, the Chapel of King Henry VII. at Westminster, may form some idea of the general character of this Chapel of Edgar in its finished state.

Local memory and tradition generally preserve some traces, however dim or distorted, of an archi-

[1] Vide Capgrave's *Chronicle*.

tectural work of great magnitude and beauty, but it is a strange fact that this one had utterly faded out of knowledge save for some scattered and obscure notes in the pages of the old county antiquaries, which contained no hint of its identity.

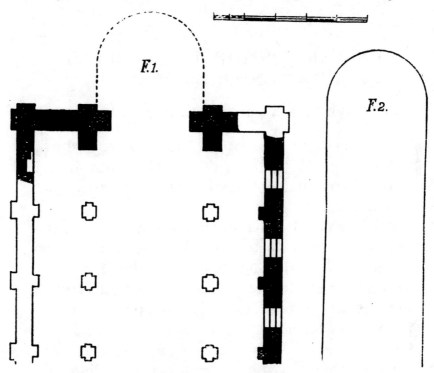

FIG. 1.—PLAN FROM PHELPS'S "SOMERSET," REPRODUCED IN WARNER'S "GLASTONBURY."

Shewing in dotted lines the reminiscence of an eastward Lady's, or Retro-Chapel, thought to have been built by Abbot Adam de Sodbury in the early part of the fourteenth century.

Two different states are shewn, both lettered 'F' by these authors, and here numbered 1 and 2. No. 1 shews by scale a projection from the retro-choir of 30 feet; whilst No. 2 gives a total length of 95 feet. This is called by Warner, "the chapel according to its original proportions." The two measurements are approximately harmonised by Leland's record of the lengthening of the choir by Abbot Monington to the extent of two bays, and the throwing out of his new retro-choir to the east, which would absorb about two-thirds of the length of this chapel.

DISCOVERY OF THE EDGAR CHAPEL, GLASTONBURY ABBEY:

AN ACCOUNT OF A PSYCHOLOGICAL EXPERIMENT

THE following is the story of the discovery which, in 1908, caused a good deal of public interest, and provided the archæological world with an object of attention.

Although known to a small circle of friends of the writer and his colleague in the research, and to the Secretary of the Society for Psychical Research, who was intimately acquainted with both, and in touch with them at the time, no publication of the circumstances has yet been made, and this was withheld largely for reasons more or less personal to the writer, though the intention had always been to make known the facts whenever the time should seem ripe for the disclosure.

The entire record has been preserved, and the testimony of both the writer and his friend being available, as well as the contemporary evidence of the Secretary of the S.P.R., it will be seen that the matter stands on a fairly good basis in respect of documentary witness.

For reasons of convenience, initials will be used

in the ensuing account. F.B.B. will denote the writer, and J.A. his friend, John Alleyne.

In anticipation of an appointment to the position of Director of Excavations at Glastonbury Abbey on behalf of the Somerset Archæological Society, of which he was a member, F.B.B. had, during 1907, devoted considerable time to the study of the ruins and their history, and to that of the older religious foundations, and in this J.A. assisted him. Most of the surviving accounts of the Abbey were gone through, both the works of the mediæval writers and those of the seventeenth, eighteenth, and nineteenth centuries, with the fragments collected by them from older sources. Among the first, the works of William of Malmesbury, Adam de Domerham, William Wyrcestre, and John of Glaston, were examined, whilst Leland was not overlooked, and the later antiquaries, Hearne, Dugdale, Hollar, and Stukely, had their share of attention. Following these, Browne-Willis, Britton, Carter, Collinson, Phelps, Kerrich, and Warner, were consulted, and finally some careful attention was bestowed on the modern antiquaries, Parker, Freeman, and last, but not least in importance, Professor Willis, whose *Architectural History* was the standard book of reference on the subject during the latter half of the nineteenth century, and still remains of the greatest usefulness to students.

Glastonbury Abbey having passed out of private hands into the custody of a body of Trustees, acting on behalf of the National Church, it was hoped that a greatly increased opportunity for research and excavation would ensue. All published plans of the Great Church had been necessarily very incomplete, in the absence of visible remains and the lack of trustworthy evidence from documents. In particular the following features were in doubt:

1. The form of the retro-quire, and eastward termination of the Abbey Church.

2. The question of a north porch to the nave, and its probable position, if it existed.

Retro-quire and Chapels.

In 1866 Professor R. Willis published his invaluable *Architectural History*, being the substance of a communication he had made to the Archæological Institute in the year previous. He devotes two pages (40, 41) to a discussion of the number and arrangement of the chapels east of the processional path in the retro-quire, and arrives at the conclusion that they were five in number. And in his plan (Fig. 2), which appears as a frontispiece to his work, he shows these five, the central one projecting about 12 feet. On p. 43 he says:

" As Bere is also said to have built Edgar's Chapel at the east end of the church, it is probable that this chapel was one of those that we are considering, and that Bere fitted it up and completed it. The complete eradication of the east wall of the church in the centre may be accounted for by supposing that the central chapel projected eastward, as I have shown in the plan, and that this chapel was Edgar's; for if it had been only one of the ordinary chapels it would not have been worth mentioning as a distinct building."[1]

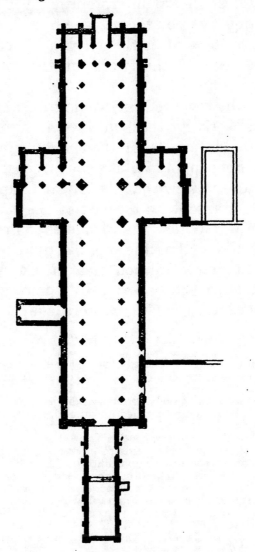

FIG. 2.—PROFESSOR WILLIS'S PLAN.

[1] *Cf.* Leland's *Itinerary.* " Abbate Beere buildid Edgares Chapel at the Est End of the Chirch, but Abbate Whiting performed sum part of it."

Professor Willis's conjecture represents the largest or most liberal interpretation yet placed by any antiquary upon the passage from Leland—which, it may be said, is the only known contemporary evidence of this work of the last two Abbots.

Parker,[1] who reviewed the whole subject of the plan in his work for the Somerset Archæological Society (see his article in their *Proceedings* for 1880), does not support Willis's conclusions, inclining rather to the view that the Edgar Chapel was in the south transept, to the east of the *nave*, but it is within the writer's knowledge that Professor Freeman believed that the original quire, which, before Monington's addition of a fifth and sixth bay, must have been shorter by some 39 feet, was furnished with a large eastern chapel, prob-

[1] See paper by James Parker, M.A., in 1880 volume of *Som. Arch. Proc.*, p. 101, where he says, speaking of the Edgar Chapel: "The question is, What did Leland mean by the 'est end of the chirch'? Does he mean the choir? Of course, I cannot say that he does not. But there are two considerations. The first is the view preserved by Stukely, taken by his friend Mr. Strachey before the Abbot's House was pulled down, and, as I understand it, some few years before 1723. In this a larger portion of the second chapel in the south transept remains than now, and it is lettered 'Edgar Chapel.' He seems to have obtained his name from hearsay, and possibly no importance ought to be attached to the tradition by itself. The other consideration seems to me more worthy of attention, and may perhaps support the tradition, where it is said in the next paragraph which Leland gives in reference to Abbot Bere, that he 'arched' on both sides, the east part of the church."
Parker proceeds to argue that this arching probably refers to the east end *of the nave*, not of the choir, and that if so, then Edgar's Chapel belongs to the same work, and would thus be connected with the transept also. "And there," says Parker, "it is placed in the only engraving which gives the name." "On the whole," he concludes, "I think it must be left an open question as to what Abbot Bere built; at least, that the evidence is not sufficient to justify putting Edgar's Chapel *at the east end of the choir*."

ably a Lady-chapel, and that this may have been of quite considerable dimensions and even co-extensive in total length with the plan as given by Willis. But this view does not appear to have gone farther than a mere expression of opinion verbally given at a meeting in the Abbey, and the writer only heard it quoted as a reminiscence some time after the discovery of the Edgar Chapel.

It appears to have been put forward as an explanation of the curious diagram given in Phelps's *Somerset*, where a plan of the church is published, showing in dotted lines a short projection at the point where Willis shows his chapel, and this is given a semicircular or apsidal end.[1] Phelps calls this the " Lady's Chapel." And in the corner of the same sheet this author gives another long rectangular diagram, again with a semicircular end, which Warner, who reproduces the plan, calls the " Chapel according to its original dimensions." The apse being the constant feature, these additional dimensions would be to the west, and would answer to the difference in the former and the latter dimensions of the quire which Monington lengthened in 1344-5. And it will be clear that some such reasoning may have guided Parker or Freeman to the tentative conclusion mentioned, and have assisted Willis to form his definite theory of a slight prominence in the central chapel of the later retro-quire.

Among the documents which have been re-covered whose period is that of the immediate

---

[1] See Fig. 1, p. 5.

post-Reformation, is one which would have been readily accessible to Willis and others, and which is preserved by Phelps and copied by Warner in his *Glastonbury*, published in the twenties of the last century. This is a transcript of a report made to Queen Elizabeth by a Commissioner, who was sent to make an inventory of the Abbey buildings, and he gives a series of measurements of the principal parts of the monastery, including the Abbey Church, as to which he says:

" The great church in the Aby was in length 594 as followeth:

The Chapter House, in length, 90 foot.
The Quier, in length, 159 foot; in breadth, 75 foot.
The bodie of the Church, in length, 228 foot.
The Joseph's chapell, in length, 117 foot."

In the seventeenth century we have the bare statements of Hollar and of Hearne, that the total length of the Abbey Church was 580 feet.

All the measures given by the Elizabethan Commissioner are very excessive, and perhaps for that reason, as well as for the confusion of idea suggested by the association of the Chapter-House measure with those of the Church, they have been rejected, or not regarded, by modern antiquaries. In like manner the bare statement of Hollar and Hearne, being without any description of what buildings were to be included in their measure, has not been taken into account.

Professor Willis's review of the probabilities of the plan of the east end seemed conclusive as regards the existence of five chapels in a row on the east wall of the retro-quire, for the construction he places upon William Wyrcestre's description must be admitted to be most reasonable, fortified as it is by the record of Wild's plan (1813), in which the bases of two piers with fragments of wall attached and running eastward are shown in precisely the position required as partitions for the forming of the three central chapels of the five.

These piers had evidently been recently discovered, and are figured in Britton's *Architectural Antiquaries*, vol. iv., p. 195. But all trace of them has been cleared away, and, as Willis himself says (*op. cit.*, p. 42):

" Unfortunately, the practice in respect to these ruins until the beginning of this century and later was always to remove not merely the wrought stones, but also to eradicate the foundations. And although the remains have been for many years protected from this kind of destruction, THERE IS NO HOPE LEFT OF RECOVERING ANY DETAILS OF PLAN BY EXCAVATIONS." (*Capitals mine.—F.B.B.*)

So the matter remained until, in 1903-4, the Archæological Institute decided to make Glastonbury the scene of its labours, and Mr. (now Sir William) St. John Hope was deputed to prepare a paper for their annual meeting.

Mr. Hope, having in mind such plans as Abbey Dore, where four chapels appear against the east wall of the retro-quire, reviews William Wyrcestre's statement in this light, and places on his words an alternative construction such as would be correct if that writer had been habitually precise in his descriptions. But he is not precise, and a general inspection of his writings will sufficiently show that he has a peculiar method of representing facts where number, series, locality, or dimension are involved.   In the present instance he says:

"IN ORIENTALI PARTE ALTARIS GLASTONIE.

" Spacium de le reredes ex parte orientali magne altaris sunt 5 columpnæ seriatim et inter quamlibet columpnam est capella cum altare."

Mr. Hope thought that Wyrcestre counted each respond as a whole column, which would mean three whole columns and two responds or piers engaged with the walls north and south, suggesting, of course, four chapels only. He caused trenches to be cut east and west along the site of his supposed central dividing wall, and one north and south immediately outside the east wall of the retro-quire and across the gap where the central chapel of Willis ought to have been.   But nothing turned up which to his mind was indicative of an extension of building beyond the line of the two remaining fragments of walling marking the eastward end of the retro-quire, and his conclusion is definite—that there was not, and could never have been, any such extension of a central chapel.   And he claimed to have found support for his view of a mid-partition giving a total of four, and not five, chapels, through the confirmatory results of his excavation.   Such was the position in 1907 when the writer commenced his studies, and it will readily be seen that no prospect of success could reasonably be expected to attend further research by excavation beyond this point.

All the evidence was sifted and discussed by F.B.B. and J.A. F.B.B. attached perhaps as

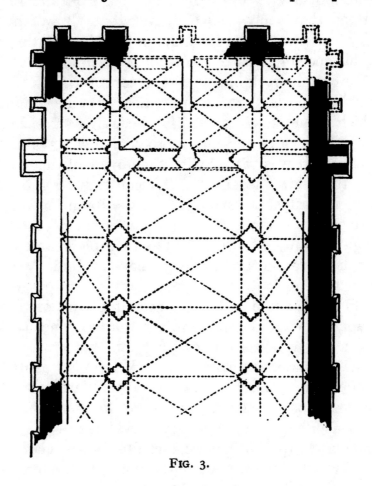

FIG. 3.

little weight to the conflicting records of a longer measure as had those who went before him. But he distinctly preferred Willis's solution to others, as there was no gainsaying the significance of

Wild's plan with its two intermediate column-bases. And instinctively he felt, as his friend also felt, that the question was not solved, the last word not said. More than once, the feeling returned that a chapel which was thought worthy of special mention by Leland, and which, according to his account, was the work of two Abbots, must have been a work of some importance.

Still, nothing came uppermost in the mind which would tend to modify the writer's respect for Willis's view, nor, indeed, to challenge its probability. It was rather with the object of defending this view, as against the contradictory one more recently put forward, that the intention was formed to examine, as soon as circumstances might permit, the site of Wild's twin piers, and to dig deep around the spot in the hope of finding yet some trace of footings characteristic of a crypt; for Wild noted these as being " probably part of the crypt," and it did not appear that anyone had taken the trouble to investigate this matter.

Wild's plan, incorporated in Britton's " Antiquities," may be regarded as a standard work. In this respect it claims greater weight than others such as Phelps's or Stukeley's, which are vague and inaccurate. Warner copies Phelps, and claims a fourteenth-century Lady-Chapel at the east, but neither Britton nor Stukeley, whose plan is two hundred years old, supports his view. Warner's note is quoted by Professor Willis (ref. to p. 31 of his *Architectural History*).

PRINCIPLES AND METHODS OF PSYCHO-LOGY APPLIED TO ARCHÆOLOGICAL RESEARCH

IT has been said that the great distinction between East and West in the matter of learning has been that whilst Western science deals with phenomena and builds upon deductions from observation of external things, Eastern wisdom looks always inwardly, seeking to find the answer to all enigmas of creation in the mind of man. The one develops the logical faculty, often, perhaps, at the sacrifice of the imaginative functions; whilst the other follows the intuitive powers, not regarding logical rules. But, as a matter of fact, neither method can be employed to the exclusion of the other, and any great discovery of Western science will be found the outcome of interaction between the two principles. It had always been clear, however, to the writer that the part played by the intuitive or, as Myers would say, subliminal powers of the mind is habitually set aside by the orthodox naturalist, who is apt to see little beyond his specimens and what can logically be inferred from them. And archæological research has been in such a manner hidebound, and, it must be admitted, with some reason; for, as a comparatively

2

young science, it has had to protect itself against many a foolish fantasy launched by a half-instructed or over-enthusiastic devotee. To describe these as " vain imaginations " would be correct, as the word " vain " is a sufficient qualification, but the writer at all times deprecates the use of the noble word " imagination " in the debased sense of a mere fantasy. Imagination is a great gift, a Divine power of the mind, and may be trained and educated to receive and to create only that which is true. And this, maybe, is the secret of much of the spiritual understanding and wisdom of the East.

But we Western folks think it unpractical to cultivate this gift. We have no system for training it, and our bourgeois habit of mind despises it. In our slipshod way, we say of anything not founded on fact, "It is all imagination," and similarly we are wont to misuse the term " illusion " by employing it to characterise positive delusion.

The training of the imaginative faculty upon scientific lines and its application to archæological research had long been a favourite notion of the writer's, and he and J.A. had many a talk on the subject; but the difficulty was as to the method most likely to secure the results at which they aimed.

What was clear enough, however, was the need of somehow switching off the mere logical machinery of the brain which is for ever at work combining the more superficial and obvious

things written on the pages of memory, and
by its dominant activity excluding that which a
more contemplative element in the mind would
seek to revive from the half-obliterated traces
below.

And it occurred to F.B.B. that in the faculty
of automatism which his friend was believed to
possess, but which he had never used deliberately
(it had operated once or twice in his life spontaneously), there might be found the key to success
in this direction. F.B.B. was a member of the
Society for Psychical Research. Both he and J.A.
were intimate with Mr. Everard Feilding, Secretary
of the Society, who had been greatly interested in
J.A.'s account of certain phenomena of automatism
which he had experienced. And E.F. had been
present at one or two experiments in the calling
of these powers into play.

Before entering upon the actual narrative of
the discovery in connection with Glastonbury, it
must be further premised that neither F.B.B. nor
J.A. favoured the ordinary spiritualistic hypothesis which would see in these phenomena *the
action of discarnate intelligences from the outside
upon the physical or nervous organisation of the
sitters.* They would regard such a view as something like a reversal or turning inside-out of the
truth. But that the embodied consciousness of
every individual is but a part, and a fragmentary
part, of a transcendent whole, and that within the
mind of each there is a door through which Reality
may enter as Idea—Idea presupposing a greater,

even a cosmic Memory, conscious or uncon-
scious, active or latent, and embracing not only
all individual experience and revivifying forgotten
pages of life, but also Idea involving yet wider
fields, transcending the ordinary limits of time,
space, and personality—this would be a better
description of the mental attitude of the two
friends.

The following may be quoted as indicating
F.B.B.'s temper of mind and feeling at a time
closely following the date of the experiments he
made with J.A. It may be found as a passage in
the Illuminated Address which he prepared for,
and which was accepted by, the Queen on her visit
as Princess of Wales to the Abbey in 1909, and
was conceived as a part of the " lovynge Greetinge
of yᵉ monkes of Glaston to theyre Prince and
Princesse. xxii Jun: Aº Mcmix." This extract
runs as follows. It was not automatic, but was
doubtless influenced to some extent by a strong
feeling in more than one quarter that Glastonbury
would be renewed as a centre of spiritual realisa-
tion and reconciliation between the various racial
elements in these islands and their distinctive
religious expressions, not yet co-ordinated (see the
writer's article on " Glastonbury " in the Christmas number of the *Treasury* for 1908, also an
address by Canon Masterman given in London in
the same year). Glastonbury, as is well known,
was a centre of pilgrimage from all parts of the
world. In most ancient times it was compared
with Rome and Jerusalem:

" For yᵉ past dyeth not but slepeth, nay ffor perchaunce hit wakyth and hit ys they of yᵉ present who doe slepe and dreme. Hit ys euen as a ffar countrie ffrom yᵉ which they heare tydynges: Yet men will fare vnto londes ffarr distant and yᵉ weelth hath bene theyr guerdon euen soe wayteth euer ffor man yᵉ treasure of yᵉ wisdom of past tymes and yeeldeth her vnto yᵉ loue whych seekyth and ys ne wearyed; soe schal yᵉ memorie of oldetyme thinges be reuealyd and of Glaston hit ys sayd yᵗ when yᵉ tymes ben ripe yᵉ glorye schal return: May hit bee euen soe Gracious Prince and Princess ÿn youre tyme."

Then yᵉ grasse schal bee as glasse
And yᵉ schal see yᵉ mysterie
Deepe downe hit lyes ffrom pryinge eies
And safelie slepes, while vigil kepes
                Yᵉ Company.

(Nowe doe) yᵉ dry bonys stir and shake
And eche to eche hys fellowe seekes
Soone comes agayne what once hath bene
And Glastonys glory shal be seene.

These verses were evolved one day in automatic writing. What their origin neither F.B.B. nor J.A. know—neither can recall having read them. Owing to their beauty and suggestiveness, they were incorporated in the Address in a form slightly modified from the original.

ON AUTOMATISM

THE essential objection to the methods and prac-
tices of the spiritualists, and the ground of that
instinctive repugnance which is normally felt
towards these methods, is undoubtedly that they
imply a surrender of the will and powers of self-
control to activities which, for good or evil, are
outside the personal sphere of the medium.   The
higher spiritual gifts are those in which the reci-
pient acts as a conscious participator in the act
of transmission.   Between these two extremes is
a class intermediate in nature, which is apparently recognised by St. Paul in the first Epistle
to the Corinthians,[1] the typical instance quoted
being that of the " gift of tongues " whose exercise, whilst not discouraged by him, was nevertheless noted as of inferior value, since it did not
tend always to the edification of the Church.   But
it was one phase of a form of inspiration then
known, probably as a common phenomenon, and
there can be little or no doubt that it was accompanied by others of a similar sort, and that in-
spirational writing was possibly one of the most
ordinary of these.   The one necessarily follows
from the other.   There is even a possible element

[1] See flyleaf.

of the kind to be weighed in any satisfying theory of Biblical inspiration, and the prophetic utterances connected therewith, and it will have to be considered fairly and apart from theological preconceptions.

It is clear from the chapter in Corinthians (1 Cor. xiv.) that in the exercise of the gift of tongues the speaker generally knew little or nothing of the meaning of what he was saying, though it is not necessary to assume that the utterance was beyond his control. But it implies the action of what, in modern language, has been spoken of as a supraliminal part of the mind, when, to quote the Apostle, " the understanding is unfruitful."

The exercise of automatism—a controlled automatism—in the production of writing seems to the author a reasonable parallel, and, where the result is capable of ready interpretation, there, according to the Apostolic dictum, is the hope of " edification " by its means. And for those prepared and ready for its exercise the gift of prophecy in those days awaited manifestation through them. And it is not necessary to suppose that the gifts then bestowed were unique, in the sense that they were afterwards to be withdrawn for all time. On the contrary, it is quite clear from Scripture itself that a great revival of them was to be expected in later days, as Peter says in Acts ii. 17, quoting the prophet Joel:

" *And it shall come to pass in the last days, saith God, I will pour out My Spirit upon all flesh : and your sons and your daughters shall prophesy, and your young men shall see visions, and your old men shall dream dreams.*"

Are we not led to believe that there is no limita-
tion to the " liberal gifts " of the spirit nor to the
variety in the nature of the spiritual gifts which
may be exercised ?   They may be concerned with
any possible branch of mental activity, and all
new ideas, whether in art, science, philosophy,
politics, religion, or what not, must be held to be
included.   Nor need the manner or method of
such inspiration concern us as of primary importance, however unusual such may chance to appear.
The one test is the quality of its message, whether
it be truthful or otherwise, edifying or lacking in
helpful qualities.   If a message of this nature be
found true, it cannot be dictated by a spirit of
falsehood; if sane, then not by insanity; if whole-
some and moral, then not by a vicious or depraved
intelligence.   Men do not gather grapes of thorns,
or figs of thistles.

The germination of new and profitable ideas in
the mind may in this respect be brought about,
firstly, by a suitable system of mental exercise
and culture; secondly, by a willingness to hold back
all mental preferences and preconceptions, and to
restrain also the surface activities of the brain, so
that the channel of pure " idea " which resides in
the subconscious mind may be maintained, and
the finer activities allowed to percolate.   Then
surely may be hoped for the reaction of those
energies sent forth by previous effort of the mind
and will, and ideas will flow back, not singly and
alone, but accompanied by a spiritual reinforce-
ment which may include elements new and of

great value, from sources beyond the ken of the individual mind.

These new elements may be of all conceivable kinds, moving instinct, intuition, imagination, affection, or will. They may be vague and abstract, or tinged, as in dreams, with a vivid sense of personality; dispassionate or pulsing with new enthusiasms; lighting the intelligence, or moving in the dark region of the subliminal mind —in this case perhaps incapable of being evoked save by automatism or the telepathy of other minds. From some inward and mysterious fount they come, borne in upon us by dynamic impulse carrying with it the fruition of memories and experiences long dormant and inaccessible to us, though within the range of the spiritual intelligence which is the Directive power. Man is a very complex being, and although, spiritually speaking, he lives and acts in relation with his fellow-men in, and by virtue of, his memories, personal and ancestral—for what are character and conscience but the fruition of all those memories and experiences which are his own or those of every pre-natal element in him ?—yet, may it not be that when released from physical conditions, as at death, there will take place some dissociation of the strata of his personality, the mere brain-record, the husk, the mechanism of his memories of common things, being scattered as the chaff, or shaken off as a discarded coat, whilst their fruit is garnered as new spiritual power and knowledge in the soul's æonial treasury ?

SOME NOTES ON THE SCRIPT AND ITS PUBLICATION

THE decision to publish these writings was formed after much careful weighing of all reasons for and against, and their issue at the present juncture was largely influenced by the feeling that public interest in such matters had greatly ripened since the war, and that the fruits of the author's experiment should not be withheld, since they might serve to direct that interest into a new and perhaps profitable channel.

The script produced during the fairly long period of time (from the end of 1907 to 1911, and again in 1912 and more recently) was obtained under varying conditions, and was of very varied quality. A large proportion had reference to Glastonbury and to monastic affairs and history, and of this only a part would claim to possess any sort of evidential value. Some was of private interest only, and would be useless for publication. Occasionally the attempted communication was a failure. In a few cases there were noted some very obvious misstatements. The most serious of these was in the measures first given for the Edgar Chapel, " Et Capella extensit 30 virgas ad orientem et viginti virgas in latitudine(m)."

A " virga " is a yard. The script was very obscure, and the measure was asked for again, with the result that " quinquaginta virgas " was written. A third time the confirmation was sought, and this time the " 30 virgas " was repeated. " Quinquaginta " (50) was obviously a mistake, but the repetition of the 30 virgas, though indicating a length vastly in excess of anything we had ever thought possible for this chapel, made one less inclined to dismiss it without further attention. The " viginti virgas " given once for the width seemed quite out of the question. And as the event proved, no measure approaching 20 yards for the extreme width of the chapel could then be shown to have existed. It appeared absurd, and was then and there ruled out, together with the inconsistent and excessive " quinquaginta virgas " of length.[1] This occurred at the close of the first sitting, which had been a long one. The writing was becoming less clear; the power was failing, and the sitters beginning to feel weary.

No further attempt was therefore made at the time to elucidate the measures, but it was resolved to try again on a subsequent occasion. There was a very cold spell in the early winter of 1907-8, and the attempts during this period were

---

[1] At a later date the excavations revealed a small chantry adjoining the south side, as at Gloucester Cathedral (Lady Chapel). This extends the width to 48 or 49 feet. If a similar chantry were appended to the north side (again following Gloucester) the extreme width might be close on 60 feet ("viginti virgas"). But of this nothing is known. Colonel Long's MS. plan, found in 1910, gives the 49 feet width.

mostly failures.   On the 13th December the sitting
was abandoned for this reason.   Another on the
21st produced nothing satisfactory.   Again, on
the 3rd January, 1908, when the cold was at its
height, only a few cramped and uncertain words
could be obtained, in which these were traced:

" Frigidus sum . . . memoria oportet nullum . . .
nescio quid aut quo[1] fecimus scriptum . . ."

Another and much more important cause of
failure must now be noted.   About the beginning
of 1908 certain circumstances of a rather anxious
and trying nature were affecting one of the sitters.
This produced a preoccupation of mind unfavourable to the production of automatic writing; and
it seems a well-established rule that the sitters'
minds must be placid and their mood quiescent
to obtain the best results.   On the 30th January,
1908, a further attempt was made to obtain writing, but with entire lack of success from this
cause, and all that was worth recording was a few
words, ending with the following: "Eschew self.
Something clogs the tones.   Search yourselves
straitly."
   It was not until the 19th of February that any
further really satisfactory results were attained,
and at this sitting the unspoken desire of the
sitters was met and a detailed description of the
Edgar Chapel given, including its outside measure
of width—namely, 34 feet.   But it was not until
Sitting XXXII. on the 16th June that the final

[1] For "quomodo."

confirmation came. This was in answer to a question, and it was given as follows:

"The width ye shall find is twenty and seven, and out-side, thirty and four, so we remember.—BEERE ABBAS."

At the date of this sitting, the west wall of the chapel had been located, but its length not yet ascertained, so that there was nothing to guide opinion as to this save what could be inferred from the position of the small section opened, which showed it to be probably about 20 feet in the clear of the footings, if placed centrally with the quire. Then, in response to the further question, What was the clear internal length of the chapel? came the reply,

"Wee laid downe seventy and two, but they builded longer."

And the veridical nature of these figures was shown by later knowledge. (See Table, p. 76.)

But to return to the subject of errors. At Sitting XXXVI., on the 19th September, 1908, there was given the story of a Saxon Earl, one Eawulf, or Eanwulf, who was slain by a certain Radulphus, Norman knight of the time of Turstin, first Norman Abbot. The story is quite a good one and contains what appears to be veridical matter, but it is marred by a peculiarity. Half-way through the script a strange mistake is noted. The name of Turstin is substituted for Radulphus, and the script says, "Eawulf and *Turstinus* did fight, and the Norman did slay the Saxon." Now such an error is tiresome, as it spoils the clearness of the story.   Yet, in another way, it is interesting, for the light that it throws on the mechanical action of the brain as the probable source of error in automatic writing or speaking.

It is a fact well known to those who are called upon to speak in public, or who are engaged in literary work, that unless the attention be fixed and concentrated on the subject in hand, the brain will act mechanically, causing repetition of any word recently impressed on the mental tympanum, and such word may easily be substituted for another.   Where there is fatigue, this may happen very easily.   In the case of automatic writing, the mind is relaxed, and there is probably a pre-disposition to such errors.   The example given seems a proof of it.   It seems, indeed, a matter for surprise that such mistakes are not more numerous in the script obtained by us.   On the contrary, another phenomenon has been fre-quently observed in connection with it.   This is, that at the commencement of a sitting the thread of a former communication, broken by the ter-mination of a previous séance, would be resumed almost as though no interval of time had elapsed.

It had been intended in the present work that only the veridical matter concerning the Edgar Chapel should appear in print; but the scope was enlarged by the inclusion of Johannes, whose personality seemed attractive.   Later, it was de-cided to allow the remarkable reminiscence of the " Loretto " Chapel also to see the light of day, in anticipation of further knowledge.   But readers will understand that nothing like a wholesale reproduction of the script in the author's possession would be possible. At the same time it may be clearly stated that in what is reserved there is nothing which contradicts or negatives the value of what is given, and of this the fact that the author has been able with success to follow out the indications given may be held sufficient warrant.

No apology seems needed for the quality of the "Latin" in the script, which is very much what one might imagine to be the colloquial jargon of illiterate members of the community, whose knowledge of the tongue would be chiefly confined to the service-books, or what they understood of them.

The author would here record his indebtedness to his friend J.A., not only for that cordial interest and co-operation without which the new line of research could not have been undertaken, nor this work have seen the light of day; but also for the verses he has written on the subject of Plate III., and on the final Envoi. His thanks are also due to Miss A. M. Buckton for her sonnet (Plate I.) and for many valued suggestions; to Mr. T. H. Felton for his permission to use material from the Cannon MS.; to the Council of the Somerset Archæological Society for loan of several blocks (including Plate II.); and to Mr. Edward Everard for the loan of Coney's and Stukeley's plates; also to Mr. Everard Feilding for his constant interest in the work and many helpful suggestions.

NARRATIVE OF THE WRITINGS

IT was on the 7th of November that F.B.B. and J.A. had their first sitting for the purpose of furthering the Glastonbury research. This took place at 4.30 p.m. in F.B.B.'s office. J.A. held a pencil, F.B.B. provided foolscap paper, which he steadied with his left hand, whilst placing his right lightly on the back of J.A.'s, so that his fingers lay evenly across its surface.

F.B.B. started by asking the question, as though addressed to some other person:

" Can you tell us anything about Glastonbury ?"

J.A.'s fingers began to move, and one or two lines of small irregular writing were traced on the paper. He did not see what was written, nor did F.B.B. decipher it until complete. The agreed method was to remain passive, avoid concentration of the mind on the subject of the writing, and to talk casually of other and indifferent matters, and this was done. The writing turned out to be a sort of abstract dictum—viz.:

" All knowledge is eternal and is available to mental sympathy."

Then followed:

" I was not in sympathy with monks—I cannot find a monk yet."

F.B.B. suggested that one of their living monk-friends might be a sympathetic link, and the writing was resumed. After a short interval J.A.'s hand moved and began to trace a line, ultimately making a drawing which on inspection looked like a recumbent cross, but which when examined proved to be a fairly correct outline of the main features of the Abbey Church traced by a single continuous line, but at the east was a long rectangular addition, nearly as long again as the quire, and this was given in a double line as though to emphasise it. Down the middle of the plan were written the words—

"Gulielmus Monachus." (See Fig. 4.)

Next followed what appeared to be an elaborate plan of the great enclosure of the Abbey Church, with a sketch of a central tower, with square pinnacled top, a west front or gabled façade, with two peaked turrets and a large arched light between. Across the middle of the surrounding enclosure a line was drawn, and at one point something like an ornamental turret with two curved diverging lines below appeared, and the words, " linea bifurcata "[1] were written. Then something looking like a gabled building was sketched, from which a line was traced to two rows of arches,

[1] The ancient " Book of Melchin " (now lost), quoted by John of Glaston, says of Joseph of Arimathea: " Amongst them Joseph of Marmore, named of Arimathea, receives perpetual sleep; and he lies in *linea bifurcata* near the south corner of the Oratory which is built of hurdles." " Linea," according to Ducange, means " an under-garment," and " bifurcata " would denote one slit at the sides like a shirt or dalmatic. But our script seems to suggest rather "a fork in the paths" as the place where Joseph lay.

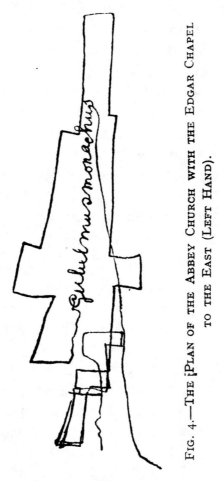

Fig. 4.—The ¡Plan of the Abbey Church with the Edgar Chapel to the East (Left Hand).

NOTE.—The drawing has all the marks of a blindfold tracing. The line is continuous, commencing at A, and the north transept is first drawn, very small. Next the line runs east, and the north-east angle of the retro-quire is traced, and, following this, the Edgar Chapel, extending east for about half the length of the quire. Here the line is drawn three times over, as though to emphasise the feature, and it then returns over the old ground, the north transept being again drawn, but larger and further removed, and the whole outline of the church is completed, to the junction south-west of the Edgar Chapel, ending with the signature GULIELMUS MONACHUS (William the Monk).

perhaps representing a cloister, and thence another straight line to a drawing recognised as being intended for St. Mary's Chapel, and approaching it from the south.   The plan of the chapel showed a large square projection (? turret) on the south, and two doors on the north side.

Q. (by F.B.B.). "What does this drawing represent?"

A. "**Guest Hall . . . St. Maria Capella . . . Rolf monachus.**"

The first drawing was now examined, and both F.B.B. and J.A. expressed a view unfavourable to the possibility of so large a chapel at the east of the church.   It was resolved to try again.

F.B.B. "*Please give us a more careful drawing of the chapel sketched just now at the east end of the great church.*"

In reply, a new sketch of the rectangular chapel was given (see Fig. 5), with an attempt to indicate the position of two smaller chapels on the north. Again the line was drawn double, and below was written the following, in cramped characters not easy to decipher:

"**Capella St. Edgar.   Abbas Beere fecit hanc capellam Beati Edgari . . . martyri et hic edificavit vel fecit voltam . . . fecit voltam petriam quod vocatur quadripartus sed Abbas Whitting . . . destruxit . . . et restoravit eam cum nov . . . multipart . . . nescimus eam quod vocatur.**

"**Portus[1] introitus post reredos post altarium quinque**

---

[1] For mediæval use of the masculine form "portus" for "porta" see Lobinell, *Hist. Brit.*, ii. 872. "Ante suum introitum fecit idem novus dux primum juramentum in introitu variere portus illius urbis vocati vulgariter Portus de Morzellos." Also in O.E. (Anglo-Saxon Psalter) "on portum" = "in porta."

passuum et capella extensit 30 virgas ad orientem et (? viginti)[1] in latitudine cum fen (?) . . . (?)."

F.B.B. *"Please repeat ; we cannot read this."*

(*Repeated.*) "Quinquaginta[2] virgas et fenestrae transomatae."

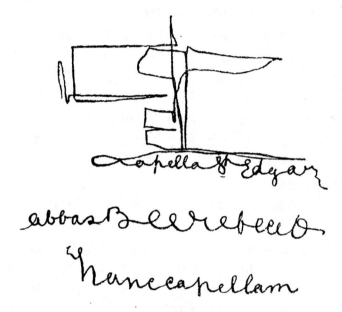

Fig. 5.—Second Plan of the Edgar Chapel as built by Beere, showing its Relative Greatness as compared with the Little Chapels of the Retro-Quire.

The line starts at the east, and again it is repeated for emphasis. The chapel is shown at first, clear of the east wall, but there is a subsequent loss of position which brings the little chapels beyond their prescribed limit and makes the plan appear confused. Below is written "Capella St. Edgar, Abbas Beere fecit hanc capellam" (Chapel of Saint Edgar, Abbot Beere built this chapel).

---

[1] A doubtful measure (see pp. 27 and 63). The writing was very weak and unsatisfactory, as though the force were waning.

[2] "Quinquaginta" is sheer nonsense, and moreover inconsistent with the measure already given. The writing was getting weaker and the difficulty increasing, and it seemed that the sitting had probably been unduly lengthened, to the physical exhaustion of the sitters.

F.B.B. *"Please give length again."*

A. " 30 virgas . . . et fenestrae (cum) lapide horizontali quod vocatur transome et vitrea azurea; et fecit altarium ornat(um) cum auro et argento et . . . et tumba ante altarium gloriosa aedificavit ad memoriam Sanct . . . Edgar. . . ."

F.B.B. *"Which Abbot did this?"*

A. "Ricar(d)us Whitting. . . . Ego Johannes Bryant monachus et lapidator."

This concluded the sitting.

SITTING II.   11th November, 1907, 1 p.m.

" The material influences were at fault when last . . . I think active influences were overpowering my will. Those monks were anxious to communicate. . . . They want you to know about the Abbey. They say the times are now ripe for the glory to return and the curse is departing. I do not know about these things. They have been wishing to influence you for a long time, and they have been (endeavouring to ?) reproduce things in your minds."

Here the influence changes.

" Benedicite. Go unto Glaston soon. Gloria reddenda antiqua. Laus Deo in saecula seculorum. Nubes evaserunt . . . memoria rerum manet et red . . . Ecclesia catholica extensit et comprehensit latera (*sic, ? latentia*) vera et res occultas sapientibus.

" JOHANNES."

SITTING III.   13th November, 1907.

Writing commenced without any direction by sitters.

" I think I am wrong in some things. Other influences cross my own. . . . Those monks are trying to make themselves felt by you both. Why do they want to talk Latin ? . . . Why can't they talk English ? . . . Benedicite. Johannes. . . . It is difficult to talk in Latin tongue (*repeated, being illegible*). Seems just as difficult to talk in Latin language."

" Ye names of builded things are very hard in Latin tongue—transome, fanne tracery, and the like. My son, thou canst not understande. Wee wold speak in the Englyshe tongue. Wee saide that ye volte was multi-partite yt was fannes olde style in ye este ende of ye choire and ye newe volt in Edgares chappel. . . . Glosterfannes (*repeated*). Fannes . . . (*again*) yclept fanne . . . Johannes lap . . . mason."

Q. " *What is meant by ' lap mason ' ?*"

A. " Lapidator . . . stonemason."

Having this signature " Johannes " now again repeated, F.B.B. felt curious to know how far this dramatisation or memory of a personality might be developed.

Q. by F.F.B. " *Tell us more about yourself.*"

A. " I . . . died in 1533." (*Repeated because almost illegible.*) " Yn 1533 obitus . . . curator capellae et laborans in mea ecclesia pro amore ecclesiae Dei . . . sculptans et supervisor . . . yn Henricum septem[1] . . . anno 1497 et defunctus anno 1533."

NOTE ON THE FIRST THREE SITTINGS.

We observe in these communications an individual tone, as of a directing influence, at first manifesting without intermediate links, but almost immediately yielding place to the monkish elements introducing themselves as " Gulielmus Monachus," " Rolf Monachus," and " Johannes Bryant." There appears something like a clash of intention, a strain which reacts on the physical

---

[1] *I.e.*, in the reign of Henry VII.

condition of the sitters, and which seems to account for the rapid exhaustion of power towards the end of the first sitting, and the consequent lack of clearness and consistency in the results.

In the second sitting the directive agency speaks of the monks as " active influences "—an expression to be noted. And it is explained that " the material influences were at fault." Then in the third sitting we get, " I think I am wrong in some things. Other influences cross my own."

It seems very much like a man trying to make a trunk call on a telephone, who is worried because the local office will either persist in switching him off at critical moments, or else because the wires are out of order and imperfectly isolated, so that fragments of other conversation are interjected.

When we come to consider the matter of the monkish communications, under the name Johannes, we are at once confronted by the question, " Is this a piece of actual experience transmitted by a real personality, or are we in contact with a larger field of memory, a cosmic record latent, yet living (the " eternal knowledge " of the first writing we record), and able to find expression in human terms related to the subject before us, by the aid of something furnished by the culture of our own minds, and by the aid of a certain power of mental sympathy which allows such records to be sensed and articulated ?

As to this, it is too early to dogmatise, but in either case room must be left for the presence of a Directive Power accessible to man, capable of stimulating and energising dormant consciousness, and directing it into such channels as man has developed for its reception and expression.

SITTING IV.   19th November, 1907.

The result was interesting, but contained nothing important as regards the Abbey.

SITTING V.   22nd November, 1907.

A further plan was produced of the general range of Abbey buildings, signed " Johannes." This was followed by a short script as here given:

"When you dig, excavate the pillars of the crypt, six feet below the grass—they will give you a clue. The direction of the walls . . . eastwards (*this word might almost as easily have been ' westwards,' or even ' outwards,' and it was so ill written that nothing could be decided from it*) . . . was at an angle . . . clothyards twenty seven long, nineteen wide."

It would have been just as easy to read the last as "thirteen." The pencilled original of the plan is preserved, but not the script, as it was not regarded as of value at the time, but the mention of the " walls at an angle," referring, as it would appear, to some part of the chapel whose dimensions are in the context, is an interesting point.

The mention of the crypt seemed simply the mentality of the sitters—a reflex of their study of Wild's plan. It is again referred to, however, in later writings.

SITTING VI. 26th November, 1907.

F.B.B. "*Perhaps Johannes will tell us something more ?*"

A. "Johannes Bryant is striving for the glory of Glaston. There is much under the grass deep down and unrifled. The east of St. Mary's has a vault under the stairs and under the nave there are vaults[1]—the destroyers feared, and the ruin of the walls hid the entrance in. Under the tower the volt is perfect, and many names of those buried therein very deep down."

Q. "*Where should we commence to dig ?*"

A. "The east end. Seek for the pillars, and the wall(s) at an angle. The foundations are deep."

SITTING IX. 30th December, 1907.

Commencement of writing quite illegible.

" . . . (the) end of the time approaches. The year is big with issues and Glastonbury will engage much of your attention. . . .

"JOHANNES, MONACHUS."

"Wait, and the course will open in the spring. You will learn as you proceed. We have much to do this season. . . ."

" . . . The chapel of Our Lady of Glaston—type of spiritual things which are not manifest to you. The changes need not alarm you. The reconstructions will be more perfect. Let the State fall in ruins and the outward garments of Faith perish—fear not!"

" . . . For greater things will rise into being—great nations and great ideals. We work for it. Be willing, and strive not against the tide. Up on the crest and prosper. All will work for the best. . . . The spark will live thro' the rains and re-light dead fires, fire which is still fire but with purer flame. We cannot hasten the time,

[1] It is most improbable that any are remaining at this day. The eighteenth century probably saw the last of them, but this may not be in the sphere of cognisance which we are here touching.

but it is sure and is not delayed. You are between two influences. Earth and spirit mingle not. Losing earthly
grasp leaves you without earthly support. Hold fast to
earth's duties. Work as men for man's meat. Keep open
ears for spiritual help and whisperings. Assimilate and
combine both forces. Stand in the market-place and cry
your wares, but listen for the still small voice in the silence
of your chamber. Work in the sun. Listen in the
starlight. . . ."

Both F.B.B. and J.A. expressed a good deal
of surprise at the nature of the first part of
this communication, as any idea of impending
revolution in Church or State had been utterly
remote from our minds and not in any way the
subject of conversation. The passage was an
intrusion and a puzzle. But we did not regard
it as of any special interest; more as a curiosity
for which a psychological explanation was lacking.

Later there occurred more such intrusions,
pointing with increasing definiteness to the nature
of that which we were warned to anticipate, but
they belong to another story and have no connection with the discovery of the Edgar Chapel.
Hence the record of many sittings will be omitted,
and we pass to the nineteenth, held 19th February,
1908, after a visit to the Abbey. F.B.B. had not
yet received his appointment, but was steadily
preparing, and at the moment was engaged in
working out the probable appearance of the approaches to the central chapel of the retro-quire,
and the work of Bere's time had been discussed.

N.B.—All the 1907 sittings were at Bristol.
The next to be recorded (Sitting XIX.) was held
at Glastonbury.

SITTING XIX. 19th February, 1908. At Glaston.

" The arche is flatte—three ells from side to side—ten feet high—all panellae. All ye midst of ye est ende was panellae and the grete chappell was[1] . . .

" . . . we have told you long tyme sins—panellae everywhere . . . thin walls and poore foundations in the new work.

" Two capellae north and south and between them a greate space with a tall doore in the midst, of four centres, all panelled under ye fann-tracery over ye lintel. And there were two altares on either side and much carven woode very blacke which was took away for the panellae. And the holes in ye walls were covered with the panellae so that they shewed not, and yt was all of stone very white and faire and in ye doore was a greate stairway with two windowes on either hand that did rise one above the other of equal height above ye stairway. . . . And ye stairway was divided in ye midst by a grete rail of stone so that they who went upp might not meet with they who came down ye said stair.

" And beyond rose a Capella of Edgar ye sainte, faire and high with grete windowes with transomes and between ye windowes were pillars as panellae the whych did holde ye roofe of stone vaultid very faire in panellae which were fanwise very fine much like carven yvorie and carvings ypainted in ye bosses and in ye spandrels and there was a grete windowe in ye est parte of eight lights all ye arches and ye roofe being flatte as of the period and the chamber was yflagged with tiles of many colours and in ye midst was a tumbe of silver and precious stones and pictures in the panellae over against ye est window. And ye chamber was in length seventy feet in four bayes and in width it was thirty and foure[2] . . . and the walls were thin and all of faire squared stone and newe carven soe that they who did destroy this . . . first, even before the great church.

" And soe hyt was not. There were faire steppes of marble and ye fannes over ye doore did hold a lyttel galerie

[1] At this point the sitting was interrupted, and was not resumed until eight hours later, when the broken thread was immediately taken up.

[2] *I.e.*, the exterior width.

the whych did open close on ye stairway looking down on them that passed there and a lytell windowe was above for to lyte ye chapell in ye church at back of ye two altares for hyt was darke.

"Forty and two feete was the hight of ye newe chapelle and yt was ybuttressed with faire buttresses and walls slantwise at ye cornere."

There appears throughout this communication a tendency to older forms of spelling never quite achieved, and constantly slipping back into the normal. The phrasing seems more consistently old-fashioned.

Note the further reference to "walls slantwise at ye cornere," recalling the "walls at an angle" mentioned in an earlier script.

SITTING XXIV.   5th March, 1908.

". . . Wold I could tell you of the great Est window in the gabell. It is hard to say its many parts but ye shall see it a noon. (*This is of the quire.*—F.B.B.)

"The buildings on the south side of the east end were two. One was a chapell, the other for the priest to robe in.

"Saint Edgar was buried in the window where ye see the cross. Afterwards Beer moved him to the new chapell that he builded. Chapell was like unto Wells but more faire."

This obviously alludes to Bishop Stillington's Chapel, a fan-vaulted structure of rich sixteenth-century work, now destroyed.

SITTING XXV.   10th March, 1908.

F.B.B. obtained the appointment as representative of the Somerset Archæological Society, with licence to excavate, in the month of May, 1908.

SITTING XXVII. 17th March, 1908. At Bristol.

" The time is ripe for the stones to be studied. Go ye soone."

" The corbel-stones are full large." (*This refers to a sketch reconstruction of the transept wall by F.B.B.*) " Put ye ten between each buttress."

Q. " Is the parapet right ?"

A. " The parapet is right."

Q. " What about the quire vaulting shown ?"

A. " Ye volte is welnigh righte for what ye see, but over Arthur's tombe to the Est window it was fayrer and much ygilt soe that the lightes of the Altar shold shine there-on and make a glory."

" Looke for ye ribs of the choir, plain ones and carven, and ye bosses. Some be at the East End. Enow has been left from the destroyer, just enow and no more : it was so ordained lest they should destroy for ever. Make ye yourselves a scheme—enow left everywhere."

" Why destroyed they not the walls that came to hande ? They cared not, but indeed they left it and digged deepe for stones.

" They could not an they would."

" Why left they the altar stones when they might have digged up ? say, why ?"

Q. " You say, ' Saxon, Norman, and Native, all strive together for the glory of Glaston. Can you put us in touch with any of these early influences ?"

A. " What wold they tell ye ? Their works were rude, and have departed. The Abbey is not of them—nothing save certain books—and we wold that the books were againe, only the Church as it was wont to be. We who speke are of its different orders : Gulielmus of old tyme, and Johannes later, and he who builded last—our Abbot Beere. What more is needed ? Wee point the way ; to you it is to fellow, and all that is needed is given you. Worke wyth brain and handes, and all is there. So it is ordained, for what ye desire, that is good that ye shall strive for. Wee worked in our day : ye must work in yours. Ne work, ne wages,—ne what you call honour."

Q. " It is St. Patrick's Day to-day. Can you tell us anything of his time and of his work, and St. Brigit's ? No doubt there was much in the great Library of the Abbey."

A. " Olde legends, meet for the people—but what value ? They were, and didde, much among the heathen. We know not more, save that their workes were old and very dry to rede." (*This passage is signed with a cross in a circle, and a capital letter, not clearly identified.*)

Q. " Please write your name."

A. " Reginaldus, qui obiit 1214—one thousand, two hundred and 14."

The identity of this Reginald is not clear. Bishop Reginald of Wells, who consecrated the Chapel of St. Mary at Glastonbury, died in 1191 according to the chronicles. The Chapel is said to have been completed in 1216.

The script has been retraced, as it was done in soft pencil and could not be preserved.

SITTING XXIX. 20th April, 1908.

" Gloria in excelsis tibi Deo.   Pax vobiscum, filii.

" The time is near. Dig well and those things which ye seek shall be given you but serche carefully lest ye eradicate those things that be left for your guidance. . . .

" . . . the est end will be the first, and then ye shall find proof of ye goodly towers at ye west end.[1]   Serche the ruins for the way they were finished. There is much left to guide you. . . ."

" . . . Influence man, and that which was before decreed shall aid you and they who are around you shall feel your influence and ours.

" In very truth it was a goodly church and it is said that ye of your time shall know what works we did pro gloria Dei.

[1] These were proved later.—F.B.B.

" We were mistaken in some things—all men are—but the thought that made the great church of Glaston was not bounded by ye mind and that thought must live and prevail.

" Move, work, and unceasingly persist, and in time there will be a place for what once was and ye shall know its buildings yet again as they were wont to be. The lesser works first : and then cometh one who will build the great church—a son of Glaston from beyond the sea. Even now he waits and watches. We wait and watch and hope with the knowledge that comes to men on the other side. The church is always the church, and in the great schema of the world we come soon and our instrument Glaston shall find a mighty place. . . . Thus Johannes saith."

At this point the sequence of the writing is broken by the story of Johannes going a-fishing, and lingering in the lanes. This we give in Part II.

Q. " We should like to know something of the nature of the old foundations which were found under the Quire in the 1904 excavations, also whether any light can be thrown upon the subterranean piers, their date and purpose ?"

" . . . The window was straight as we knew it, but[1] was somewhat changed by Abbot Beere when he made the chapell. Ye are right about ye end walls. Johannes saw to the building thereof for they were five years before they builded the last part because there was nothing in the coffers—so the church was perfect without the new parts.

" What was it Beere performed ? We will remember. The olde church had a chapell going east like to Edgar's and the corners were cut off most like. The foundations ye mean remain. We know but that which we heard and that which they who followed after did, we know not, save only we can enquire.

" Beere, Abbot, is not with us now. He has a work to

---

[1] The sitting was interrupted here, and resumed later with a repetition of the words " as we saw it, but."

perform.   There are others who build in your England and he hath to lead them as they should be led.   They who builded in our day and were masters, lead ye now.

"ROBERT.   ANNO 1334.   GLASTON."

NOTE ON SITTING XXIX.

The blending of influences is again very marked, but the dominant thought is that of one of the inmates of the great abbatial House.   The signature "Robert" (anno 1334) does not help us. This was the year that witnessed the election of John de Breynton as Abbot, vice Adam de Sodbury, and it was an era of great building activities.   But Robert speaks, or is made to speak, for those of an era two hundred years later, or nearly, and it is strange to find a voice from the fourteenth century recalling the "window" as it then was, and going on to describe alterations made at the beginning of the sixteenth.

And the allusion to Abbot Beere's living influence is of peculiar interest.   Among the best modern exponents of the Gothic English styles, the call of the past, and the influence of the past, is vital as an element in their work, and it is precisely in the measure in which they are able to translate the spirit of the past, that they can claim inspiration in what they strive to produce.[1] Occasionally a sincere student will obtain some mental pictures of a bygone time of singular clearness and fidelity, whence, he knows not; only that they are spontaneously apparent to him *when in a*

[1] The work of the mere copyist is not inspired.

state of mental passivity after intellectual exertion in the particular direction needed. It may be of interest here to quote an experience once related to the writer by an old friend, W., now retired from practice, but who in the 80's of the last century was responsible for a good deal of scholarly restoration work in the west country. W. was very partial to the Early English forms, and if he had a fault, it was the fault of his day, when restorers were a little ruthless, as we should think nowadays, in substituting Early English detail for the fifteenth century " vernacular " of the district. On one occasion he was called upon to undertake " restoration "—which, in this case, meant a partial rebuilding—of a decayed church in the very decayed town of I. The south wall of the nave, a work of the ordinary " Perpendicular " sort, had to be rebuilt, and he had to construct a new arcade for the aisle adjoining. Somehow he felt disinclined to do this in the fifteenth-century style, but was prompted to design afresh, in the manner of the thirteenth. And for his pillars he imagined a form of capital having rather a complex moulding. There was nothing visible to guide him, but it appealed to him as suitable. Nor was it a local type—at least, this would be the writer's recollection of the impression he derived from the drawing which W. showed him.

The capitals were provided of this pattern, the old wall was pulled down, and hidden within it and built into its substance was found *a pier-capital of a moulding identical in detail.* I myself

4

was satisfied that he had never seen any particle of this early work, and he allows me to retell the story here. As to the story of Johannes, the truant monk and nature-lover, it takes the form of an interpretation of his memory-record by another. Whether we are dealing with a singularly vivid imaginative picture or with the personality of a man no one can really decide. But later examples will elucidate the part he plays in the scheme, and it is one of much interest from the psychological point of view.

SITTING XXIX.—*Continued.*   20th April, 1908.

" Ye crypt was mere a chamber under the stairs and it was at the west end of the chapel.   It was not for sepulture and it is gone long syne by reason of the fall of the floor of ye chapel.

" Yt wasne underground and was low—a man might hardly walk sans stooping."

The work of excavation commenced shortly after the receipt of this communication.

SITTING XXXII.   16th June, 1908 (after excavation No. 4).

" All is well.   We direct your course and will continue. There is some difficulty and ye must use your own intelligence.   There are two chapels and ye must try and judge old and new.   The scheme of Abbot Monington gave one, and under the church are remains yet older.   The pillar of many shafts[1] was in the midst between the buttress and

[1] There is a sketch of this pillar given in the 1908 volume of the *Proc. of the Somerset Arch. Soc.*   It was found by F.B.B. in Kerrich's papers in the British Museum.   Its position would fairly obviously correspond to that which the script suggests, and there is therefore nothing very remarkable about this.

the chapel wall, and the great window needed the buttress to hold hym up. Seek out the choir wall, where the arches were behind the altar, and it will be plaine. Digge for the vestries on the south choir wall—there is somewhat left here, and there is alsoe a chantry under the window by the crosse.[1]

"Judge not the wall by the foundations thereof. They are mighty but—wee have told you—thin walls were over them.[2]

"Search far for the est end of Edgar's Chapel. It is but little damaged. S. Mary and S. Andrew's Chapels, over the ends of ye choir aisles."

The only reminiscence of a retro-chapel is to be found in the plan of the Abbey embodied in Phelps's *Somerset*, reproduced by Warner. Phelps shows a dotted-line extension of the east wall of the retro-quire of nearly the same projection as Willis's plan, but in this case it ends with a semicircle—a feature impossible for anything but a Norman chapel, which here would be out of the question. In a corner of Phelps's plan appears a similar diagram, but with the rectangular part much lengthened. Both are lettered " F,"

[1] The wall of the vestry was subsequently dug for and found outside the bay of the south quire wall third from the west, where there were indications of such an appendage in the grooving of the masonry for the flashings of a lead roof, and the plinth mould had been shorn off to get rid of an inconvenient projection. The trench showed a thin wall giving a vestry about 9 feet wide.

[2] The great breadth of the footings of the rectangular part of Edgar's Chapel—about 6 feet 6 inches on the north and south walls —might easily have inspired a wrong opinion as to the substance of the walls themselves. But students of the work of this date are familiar with the fact that the flat and heavy fan-vaulted stone roofs of the Tudor period require, in addition to their external buttresses, a certain amount of interior support, which is given by building the walls as a series of hollow bays, the windows occupying the recesses, and the intermediate masses being brought out inwards, as piers or counterforts, the same being architecturally treated, so that the description elsewhere given of " piers as panellæ " is quite probably accurate, as a description of such features.—F.B.B.

and the reference table gives " F " = Lady's Chapel. Warner copies this plan, calling this latter one " the Chapel according to its original dimensions." Neither F.B.B. nor J.A. had at that time seen Warner's copy of Phelps's plan, because the copy of Warner accessible to them in the Bristol Public Library had lost this sheet. But owing to the general haziness of the plan, and its numerous inaccuracies, and the entirely impossible suggestion of a semicircular apse (in a dotted-line figure), as well as owing to the suggestion " Lady's Chapel," these records had proved the reverse of illuminating, save as inspiring a guess that the original and shorter quire might very likely have been furnished with a Lady Chapel, for use in the remote days, before the western chapel of St. Mary had been opened up and thrown into the general series by the inclusion of the " Galilee "—a work of the fourteenth century, and that this Lady Chapel had been ultimately shorn of the greater part of its length by its absorption into the new retro-quire, what time Abbot Monington caused the quire to be lengthened by two bays (about 40 feet) *temp.* 1344 or thereabouts. Such an hypothesis would entail the deduction that after the lengthening of the retro-quire in the fourteenth century, there would remain at the east end a relatively short projection—say, of 12 feet or so—and some such reasoning may well have inspired Willis's scheme (see his plan in the *Architectural History of Glastonbury Abbey*), though he rightly rejected the semicircle as an eastern finish.

Q. " Was there any crypt under Edgar's Chapel ? What were the clear dimensions of the chapel itself ?"

A. " The cript is fallen in, but the clay is not the old clay. Clear out the midst thereof, and many fragments be there. The width ye shall find is twenty and seven, and outside, thirty and four, so we remember.

" BEERE, *Abbas.*"

Q. " What was the clear internal length of the chapel ?"

A. " Wee laid down seventy and two, but they builded longer, and he who followed made new schemes for a certaine roofe in golde and crimson, very cunning. Ye must use your talents, lest they weaken. Piece by piece ye shall rebuild it and there is enow, I wot, for ye.

" Digge east beyond the beds of feathered grasses. There was a passage to the east doore in ye walle to the streete. In the midst it remaineth. There was a lodging where now is the great howse, and wee loved passages. They were safe, and the priesthood loveth secret places. There is somewhat in us that loveth mystical things, so we tell not all, but leave it to the love which seeketh and is not wearied."[1]

At the time of this writing, only the west end of the chapel had been excavated, so that the length was still a matter of complete doubt. A massive wall running north and south had been found just about in the position of that shown as a projection in Willis's plan—namely, about 12 feet east of the walls of the retro-quire, and on the farther side of this the foundations commenced at a much higher level, indicative of a later extension by Bere from this point onwards. And the whole of this cross-wall must have been Bere's

[1] The local gardeners and workmen had a story of a large covered passage which was said to run from the house or from a point close to it, and towards the Abbey, and one workman, Thyer, now dead, told F.B.B. that he had assisted the late owner, Mr. Austin sen., to fill up a part of this and to remove the flat stone coverings which he needed for his building work.

work, for it ran north and south for some 32 feet, and beyond that came the projection of its buttresses. When the continuation walls of the chapel to the east were further revealed, the clear width between their footings was about 18 feet, and as they were each about 6 feet 6 inches in width, the whole was not quite 32. So the suggestion in the script of a clear internal width to this chapel of 27 feet is by no means improbable if measured into the window recesses. As to the length given (72 feet), a total of 90 had already been spoken of, so that the 72 must represent the rectangular portion of the chapel, *plus* either the antechapel or the eastward extension only, either of which give this approximate total.

As afterwards revealed (see plan in *Som. Arch. Soc. Proc.* for 1908), the correspondence proved to be faithful, as the scale shows. Measure from the interior of the east wall of the retro-quire, which will include all the space within the antechapel of Bere's work, eastwards to the end of his rectangular walls, and the whole is close on 72 feet —viz., $12 + 5 + 50 + 5$ in approximate measures.

There were several clumps of pampas grass on the high bank, but farther east than our advance at the moment. Another fragment of script, unfortunately now lost, again referred to one of the clumps on the south side, as being just west of a large mass of masonry. This was correct. The large mass in question is that which stands up high above the rest at the south-east angle of the rectangular chapel. Again, we have the

curious and unusual suggestion of an east door
to the chapel (compare the " Portus introitus post
reredos," etc.). When, long subsequently, the
two inclined walls of the apse were revealed, the
gap in the middle was remarked. The footing on
the north side of the eastern gap was cut squarely
off, and evidently by intention, and was thus
strongly suggestive of a doorway or archway here.

In " the walle to the streete " we may perhaps
discern an explanation of the continuation of the
angular wall on the south, which runs on for a
distance not yet ascertained in the direction of
the upper part of the town, and would have passed
near the building which formerly occupied the
site of the present Abbey House.

" Use your talents. Wee guide. It is meet. Noe
worke, noe wage. All workes well. This wee tell you.
Ledde was on the roofe—ne stones, the wych cometh from
meaner buildings elsewhere. The stone tiles were high
roofes but ye chappell was flatte or thereabouts.

" As how think ye the est ende would have looked to
them who came from the green pathe in the wall ?

" . . . and ye can see right well. Dig deeper : it
needeth. Fear not. It will be clear to you ere another
night fall. Even yet there is somewhat east and south to
finde. Ye are skilled to find the stones which we put there.
All are of the chapelle that ye have noted.

" Benedicite.

" WHYTTINGE, *nuper Abbas*."

It was not until several months later that
the whole of Bere's rectangular chapel was
disclosed. The bank increased in height as we
proceeded east. But the farther we went, the
more stone we found on the south side, until at

last, at the south-east corner, a block of solid masonry was uncovered which rose several feet above the general level. And to the south of the last two buttresses on this side there came to light the trench or matrix of a small additional building, a chantry or a sacristy. These trenches were cleared and filled with solid concrete to preserve the record of the lost walls, which must otherwise have perished through the falling-in of the loose and crumbling earth.

SITTING XXXVI. 9th October, 1908.

" Ye must see owre old manor of Sharpham. There is somewhat for you there. Search it diligently, and the walls around.

" Ye church ye have found is ye one which Ina builded and it was yjoined to the olde churche by a timber passage-way and many steppys. Yt had no towre, but as it were the short arms of a crosse and ye pillars were greate and rounde as ye see. (*This alludes to an excavation in the nave.*)

" Ye roofe was woode and it was rough and rude, ne like unto our church of St. Mary.

" Would ye could digge around ye altare,[1] for there ye will find much black marble of the style ye call ' decorated.'

" We wold make ye see it—square, and as it were square buttresses with canopies and imagery, full forty feet in height, somewhat level in ye toppe, like a screene, and in ye midst a faire canopy of gilded stone in width four feet and full of fifteen feet in height ; and in front an image of Our Lady in gold and scarlet robes holding in her hands the Christ and a sceptre of power. On either side two doors with steppys leading down to the path for processions behind ye altare. Can ye not see it ? Black stone and images, and guilding in the hollow places under the ornaments. On ye south side, as we deem it, ye will find most of ye pieces and even ye tombes of Arthur and of ye two saints Edgar[2] (*sic*) all black stone with much guilding and ye effigies

---

[1] *I.e.*, the high altar of the later church.
[2] Should be " Edmund."

PLATE II.

THE EDGAR CHAPEL.

View of the completed excavations, showing Bere's rectangular chapel
of four bays, and the eastern annexe with the " walls at an angle."

cf ye Kinge and ye Queene with ye Lyons in blacke stone —nay, rather, ye Lyons were in light stone like ye bases of ye tombes.

"And ye grete east window in pannels like unto ye sides of ye choir, and very faire, with a balcony. Ye balcony was underneath ye window and from yt did lead the way to ye altare back where was an ymage of Saint Mary, of great value and very olde, which was saved from the fire long synce.

"Ego sum JOHANNES qui ex memoria rei dico—meminisco—dixi annorum 1492." (I am Johannes, who speak from memory of the matter. The time of which I spoke would be 1492, as I remember.)

SITTING XXXVII.   30th November, 1908.

"The ending of the chappel was at an angle, the sides makyng as it were a baye in the east wall there. The last bay to the east hayde an arche like unto a chancel arche and with a feather ornament, as hadde all the other arches; and the space beyond into the baye was as it were three fannes with thin pillars running up the angles and spreading toward the arche. In the three faces of the east wall were three windowes, and all this was faire made by Abbot Whitting, who lengthened Edgar's Chappel somewhat, to the extent of half a bay. . . . The fannes are flat which Whitting builded, and ye will see them how they fitted together.

"The lytell chantry was roofed in pannels by . . . Beere, and ye have found the pieces, deep cut and faire —quatrefoil with lozenges, cuspings on either side, and ye roofe as was called 'barrel' shaped—ne fannes in ye chantry."

This script was obtained before the angular walls of the apse had been found. The description generally is quite a plausible one, and there is good reason for thinking that the apse would have been finished by the last Abbot (Whiting). Some stones of the fan-work were found at the end of the year.   The " little chantry " would seem to refer to the projecting footings found between the last two buttresses on the south side.   It compares again with Gloucester Lady Chapel, where such additions are found north and south of the fourth bay from the west.

Q. " Whence came the vaulting-rib, which we have found ?"

A. " He went in the passage-way to Edgar's Chappel and the volting of like molding went with it—east of the arches behind the altare.

" Monington was used to what ye call ' decorated ' and the choir roof wasne of the newe style—ye ' perpendicular,' but the other style done after Gloster fashion."

SITTING XXXVIII.   2nd December, 1908.

" Gulielmus monachus qui in area chori requiescet[1] . . . Reginaldus.   Hee wots not what they didde but saith the olde procession path went round three corners and they builded the new window after hys tyme straight.   Ye have found the old wall before Monington.   I guess but doe not know.

" Gulielmus monk of Saint Benedict wold speke but he hath been long ded and cannot as he wold.   He of Monington Abbas qui . . . he did make the est end full square, that know I he didd, and in hym three arches and a grete screene . . . soe it was in my day, that he who followed after did enlong the window and it was full weake and they rebuilded it. . . .   He did build strong walls over ye lytell chapel of Our Ladye that then was and in them a new window and on either side he placed a walle which did continue the walls of the choire and did put in an arche and under hym a tombe on either side with the altar in the midst, and above the arche as it was two grete high windows, very narrow which did make on to the grete east window and wyth hym made a grete faire window which did light up all the choir and did fill it with glassen cleare and bright of many colours."

[1] William the monk who reposes in the quire.

SITTING XXXIX. 5th December, 1908.

" Johannes wold speke. There is (somewhat) gone from us. The olde foundations were left and they did add to them. The walls at an angle were put in by Abbot Beere when he builded the chappell and enlarged the windows. We have told ye of the high windowes and the arche under wych the tombe(s) of Edgar (*sic*) one on either side—the Elder and the Younger. The arch was ycarven very faire and panellae did rise to ye roofe, and ye volte over the Est window was ydonne in fanne worke: likewise the eastern part of ye choire was in fannes wyth a great arch as soe it was donne with panellae between."

During the summer and autumn of 1908 the work of excavation had been steadily continued. By December practically the whole of the rectangular portion of Beere's chapel had been laid bare, and proved to be of four bays, in accordance with the script. The excavation of the antechapel entirely confirmed Willis's view of the divisions of the retro-quire, and, strange to say, justified his plan in regard to the length of the central projection, for it was abundantly clear from the appearance of the two flanking walls (or, rather, their foundations) that there had been an original projection here of the same extent as he showed, and that Beere had merely taken on at this point and started his new work with a massive cross-wall at a different level. The footings of the north and south walls of Beere's chapel were about 6 feet 6 inches broad and a little over 18 feet apart in the clear. The thin Perpendicular work above would normally stand rather over the outer margin of the footings to allow of the projecting piers supporting the fans of the roof, and this would entirely justify a computation of width approaching 27 feet clear into the recesses of windows. But the total internal length on the foundations between east and west footings measured 49 feet, a dimension in itself insufficient to justify the 70 feet claimed in the script, even if it were considered that part of the breadth on the west footing, and an even larger part on the east footing must be included in the interior area of the chapel. Possibly a further 6 feet or so might be allowed for these margins, making a total internal length for the rectangular chapel of 55 feet, to which another 15 feet must be added if the measurement of 70 feet given in the script were to be justified.

But the rectangular chapel ended off with a proper finish to the east, and the two return buttresses were well marked. At this point the digging had been very deep, as the level of the bank rises steadily from west to east, and we were now about 10 feet under the grass level. The rectangular end was cleared, and before us rose a sheer face of clay without trace of any continuance. Nothing had yet been seen of " walls at an angle," and the writer scanned the face of the clay many times, trying to detect any signs of disturbance or of a further junction of building, and so matters remained till the end of December.

In the meantime a report had been prepared for the annual volume of *Proceedings of the Somerset Arch. Soc.*, and as by this time F.B.B. was fully persuaded that Hearne and Hollar are giving

us fact when they state that the total length of
the Abbey was 580 feet, he boldly drew a plan of
the excavated chapel with an addition in dotted
lines, making out the requisite dimension and
showing a polygonal annexe or apse, and this he
caused to be published in the 1908 *Proceedings*.[1]

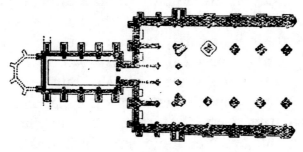

FIG. 6.

During the Christmas holidays F.B.B. again
visited the site, and on a bright sunny day looked
at the clay bank, and for the first time detected a
small squarish patch of pale brown discoloration in
the clay at a level much higher than the footings of
the chapel. He caused the face to be cut into at
this point, which was nearly opposite the southern
return buttress, and at a point about 2 feet within
the clay face the stump of a wall appeared. This
was traced and proved to run north-east at an
angle of 67 degrees from the north and south axis
of the chapel.

The ground was opened in the corresponding
position on the north side, and here a trench was
found well and truly cut in the clay, and filled
with débris of sixteenth-century freestone, tile,

[1] A facsimile of this plan was published in the *Treasury* for
Christmas, 1908.

and glass fragments, chiefly of painted work, and largely of azure blue.[1] The footing-trench was inclined at a similar angle, but instead of meeting a cross wall at east, it stopped short at the point where such a return wall should be, and this indicated that in all probability the annexe had a door in the east wall,[2] behind the reredos, suggestive of the use of this part as a feretory or relic-chamber, and this recalls almost exactly the plan of the church (collegiate) of Westbury-on-Trym, which is also furnished with a semi-hexagonal apse.

Calculating that the inner faces of the three walls of this annexe would have been designed to be more or less equal in breadth, for sake of symmetry, a line was struck across the apse at the required point, a stake put in, and a very careful chain-measure made from end to end of the whole range of Abbey buildings—*i.e.*, from the internal face of the Lady Chapel or Church of St. Mary at the west, to this point, and the measure was then found to be *precisely* 580 *feet, as given by Hearne and Hollar*. The true plan of the chapel was published in the 1909 volume of *Proceedings*, and makes an interesting comparison with the conjectural plan (see Fig. 7, p. 64).

Two years later, in the collection of Colonel Wm. Long, J.P., of Clevedon, an eighteenth-century manuscript plan of the ruins, hitherto quite unknown, came to light, and was found to show the two inclined wall-sections of the apse

---

[1] *Cf.* p. 37, line 3.
[2] *Cf.* p. 35, last line, " Portus introitus post reredos," etc.

of the Edgar Chapel. A note attached to this plan gives the extreme dimensions of the chapel as 87 feet by 49 feet. The latter would only be correct if it included the little chantry projecting on the south side. It would not represent the true outside measure of the chapel proper, which is elsewhere stated as 34 feet, and must have approximated to that width.

Eighty-seven feet is of course fairly correct as an internal measure of length, and thus substantiates the record.

SITTING XXXIX.—*Continued*.

" AWFWOLD ye Saxon hath tried, but hee knows not ye tongue. He hath somewhat of olden tyme that ye have found in ye este. He sayth hee hadde a house or housen in wattlework and a churche within the forte, ye which wee did enter when wee made Edgar hys newe chappell. Soe he sayth. And that wych is beyond the chappell, is not there a chambre, the wyche ye shall see when ye have digged full deepe. And from hym did go a passage way to the Lodge over the gate that leadeth to Chalice. Hyt is gonne full syne, wee wot. Wyth hym—the chambre— ye church was six hundred and twenty-eight feete in length inside and sixteene more outside walls, soe wee remember."

The blackened wattlework was found at a great depth in the clay near the south-east corner of the Edgar Chapel. It was examined together with other remains, and reported on by Mr. St. George Gray in the *Proceedings of the Somerset Archæological Society* for 1909. No attempt has been made to explore the site beyond the eastward limit of the Chapel. The ground is very deep, and

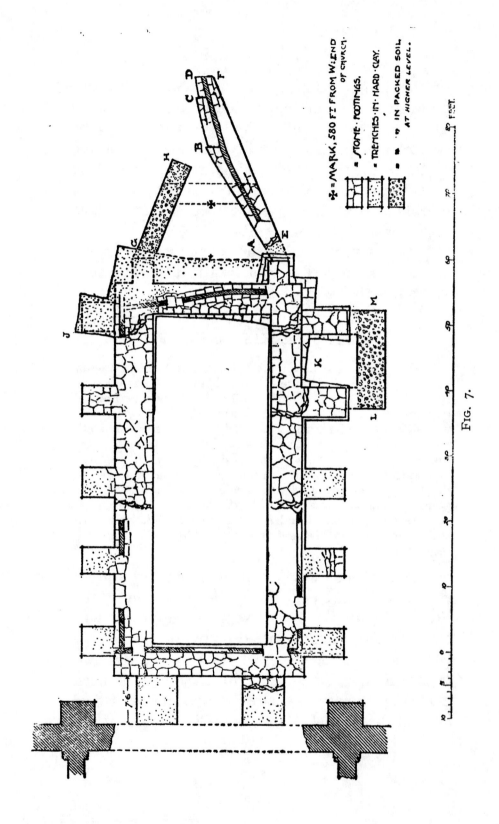

FIG. 7.

✠ = MARK, 580 FT FROM W. END
    OF CHURCH.

☐ = STONE · FOOTINGS.

☐ = TRENCHES · IN · HARD · CLAY.

☐ = IN · PACKED · SOIL ·
    AT HIGHER LEVEL.

FEET.

there are other difficulties. As the proved internal length of the Abbey with the Chapel is 580 feet, this measure of 628 feet would imply another large addition, and in the absence of any sort of evidence of its probability, it is impossible to attach the least weight to it.

"The tombe of Arthur in shining blacke stone was in front of ye altare. Ye can see hys size even now, an ye wis, in ye claye, and certain fragmentes that yet are for hym to seeke. Blacke and scarlet and golde was ye choire, save where they didde paint ye leaves in greene, and somme tyme browne where ye clausteres were. Ye windowe was much clere glasse wyth colours in ye midst under golden canopyes in ye heades of the pannels. There was under ye alare (*sic*) a chambre ye wyche ye did enter from the rear, but hee was low and smalle, and there were many buried in hym. The pathe for processions wasne needed, and soe they went not behind ye altare where ye chappells were nor behind ye greate screene under ye este windowe. The churche he was soe grete there was room enow in ye aisles and soe across ye altare in front of hym by Arthur's tombe."

Q. " As to traces of an interment behind the reredos wall. Can you tell us anything of this ?"

A. "Yee martyr was hee. They made a martyr's grave. He was not coffined, for they were but bones got by ye faithful from Bathe and Tauntone, and brought in secret. He was yplaced under ye altare, and they who pulled yt downe when Elizabeth was Queene drew hym out. They knew not who hee was, our Abbot. Ye knowe. . . . Hee who swam in ayre when hee wold not. Whytynge. They knew not. Wee deemed the altare wold stande for alle tyme."

Q. " Who desecrated the Abbey ?"

A. "My Lord Somersete. Hee cared but for golde —ne faith, ne good—Hee a Protestant, a traitor hee. A heretic was hee."

5

Q. "Is there any foundation for the legends of secret passages in and about the Abbey?"

A. "Covered ways to the corner of the cloyster by ye Prior's House. Hee is fallen in, we wot, and likewise hym that goeth to King's Gate, but somme is left. Some of ye passage at the east end ye shall finde. (*Here follows a plan.*) The Kingswaye seeke ye neare ye Gatehouse—ye cellars that wee used. Ye shall find ye passage. Ye shold seek the grete draine. Many things are therein. Ye should seeke for it.

"JOHANNES et alii.
"Permultae memoriae."

SITTING. 1st September, 1910.

The script begins in a cramped hand, very disjointed and confused. It is mostly in Latin words, and we trace the name of one John of Aller, in the rural district of Somerset ("in agros Somersetiae"), formerly a husbandman, but later a watchman at the Abbey. But he cannot tell us what he would, and the power which should recall his memories fails. "Nescio quid sum," it ends, "aut inde veni."

Then the writing commences afresh, thus:

"Ambrosius the Cellarius wold speke to ye. And hee isne a scholar. Ye binnes in ye cellar ye wot they were full of good wine, but ye cellars of ye Guesten Hall lye deeper downe.

"Ye roofe of ym[1] is but even with ye floor of hym. But I wot they have left ye little enow.

"Ye Abbot's lyttell kitchen he lay in between ye two halles, and ye cooke hadde enow to feed them on the one syde and alsoe ye guesten folk on ye other. Therefore ybuilded ye Abbot ye grete Kitchen afore ye Howse, for to make feast on grete feast-dayes. Ye olde kitchens and

---

[1] 'Them,'—*i.e.*, the cellars.

ye minte-garden wasne used much after that. Ye newe howse of ye Abbot hadde kitchens enow, and soe. . . . Know ye ye lytell cloystere ahint ye Prior's Lodging and ye Halle convent over against the Stabels of ye horses? They were near ye Guest Halle on ye syde of our Lord Abbat's Howse, and ye menne lay over them. There were foure horses, and rooms for ye guesten horses in ye same stable."

The script here deals with an area still unexcavated, as to which we have but little documentary evidence. The position of the Guest Hall may be reasonably inferred to be on the site suggested, due west from the Refectory. The statement about the kitchens seems reasonable. At this point the communication under the name Ambrosius ceases and an entirely different handwriting is noted. The script continues:

" Ricardus de Tanton, who did make ye drawings for my Abbot Bere, wold tell you that which Ambrosius can not."

We gather that the level of the ground was lowered and four cellars made for storing wine for the Guest Hall above. Next we read:

" The grete Halle was ybuilded not long syne, and ye must goe where the kitchens did joyne him to the Refectorium. Aufwold says that the convent of Arimathia was at hys southwest corner, builded long tyme since, and there was as it were a little cloystere between the Hall and the chapel where Beere did saye masse. The stabel was over aganst the Abbat's new howse which Beere builded, and which was in front of the Guest Hall but away from hym. The crypt under the new Hall was deeper downe. His roofe was near level to the floore of the vault of the Refectorium. . . .

" Goe you through the grete door at ye corner of ye Cloyster on ye est syde downe XII steppes and on through ye passage-waye. Then shall ye rise uppe ye steppes IX on ye south syde, and soe acrosse ye mint garden to the Newe Halle where was a doore, and through hym cometh a passage to the further syde and soe to the lyttel cloyster, and beyond hym the lyttel convent and ye lyttel chapel builded long time syns. And there was a grete wall to the est of all these places high and stronge, and over hym was the dormer, and beyond, the parlour beneath and the scriptorium above hym: and soe unto ye wall of ye lyttle cloystere, and after a space, a yarde and the schola with its chappel and buildings around yt . . . for ye boyes, alsoe ye changing room for ye choire who sang in ye minster.

" Ye boyes were ofttimes joyous and did playe and make a shouting, and ye Abbat sayde : ' Chide not youth in its playe, but may ye keepe them afar from ye claustre places lest they weary my devowte,'—and so ye schola was far from ye (same)."

Q. " Which was the Chapel of St. Dunstan ?"

A. " Hym on ye North syde of ye Grete Church, at ye ende, near to ye newe chappel which Bere (built)."

Q. " What was the exact length of the Church as completed ?"

A. " CCCXI[1] in passibus. CCCXI et capella nova. CCCXI in tota longitudine."

[1] The length of the mediæval " pace " was unknown to us, and would have been inferred to be the natural length of a walking " step " (in F.B.B.'s case 22 inches).

But to reduce paces to feet, or *vice versa*, is not easy by mental arithmetic, and the calculation was not made. Hence this CCCXI conveyed nothing definite.

But publication necessitated scrutiny of this statement, and, to assess the true length, reference was made to William Wyrcestre's *Itinerary*, wherein, speaking of Glastonbury Abbey (p. 292), he says:

" Longitudo navis ecclesiae monasterii continet 54 virgas vel 100 gressus "—making 54 yards=100 steps.

If 100 steps=54 yards, one step=1·62 feet. So we have our material for calculation, as follows:

1. Length of church   ..   ..   ..   311 × 1·62 = 503·82 feet
   " et capella nova " (*i.e.*, and the new chapel) (add)   90·00   ,,
                                                          ————
                                                           593·82   ,,

Q. " Please state it in feet."

A. " Pedes DCCXXXIII[1] circa."

Q. " Was there anything east of the Edgar Chapel ?"

A. " **Yes,** but not Ecclesia major. On the wall was a capella for them who came from over the hill called Chalice —a little capella, but he was not of the grete church. You have hym all.

" **We** sayd he (the church.—F.B.B.) was somewhat over three hundred passuum on the path which passeth on the north syde of hym. This I knowe. The chappell was ninety-one[2] of feet, for I did draw hym.

" RICARDUS Tª."

—an amazing result ! Elizabeth's commissioner, quoted on p. 12, says:

" The great Church in the Aby was . . . 594 feet." And our own plan (Fig. 12), based on careful measurement, yields the total 592 feet ! (The 580 feet measure discussed on p. 62 is an *internal* measure.)

[1] DCCXXXIII pedes *circa* (*about* 733 feet)—at first sight a hopelessly discordant measure, being 140 feet in excess of the first—yields on analysis an even more astonishing result. For 733 feet circa *is* 311 paces; but Romano-British paces—not mediæval ! 311 paces of 2 feet 4¼ inches is 733 feet. The true Roman pace (single) is 2 feet 5 inches—occasionally less in Britain —so we see it in this case slightly shortened. And the qualification " circa " gives us the slight latitude which the computation requires.

It is as though our question, addressed to the previous informant, had been answered by another in a literal sense, according to his own knowledge of the measure, and without reference to the monkish standards. (See note in synopsis at end of vol., *sub.* " Ell" and " Passus.")

[2] This being a foot in excess of the measure first given and found correct, we have preferred the latter in the calculation given on the last page.

TABLE OF THE VERIDICAL PASSAGES IN THE AUTOMATIC SCRIPT, SIXTEEN IN NUMBER, REFERRING TO THE EDGAR CHAPEL AND EAST END OF QUIRE

I. AS TO A LARGE RECTANGULAR CHAPEL EAST OF THE RETRO-QUIRE.

SCRIPT.	EXISTING DATA.	RESULT.
November 7, 1907. Plan of Abbey, showing oblong chapel at east end, of very large dimensions, and exterior to retro-quire, the width overlapping three of the five chapels of same. The sketch would indicate a width between 20 and 30 feet, and a length probably exceeding 70 feet.	Professor Willis's *Architectural History* shows nearest parallel, but his plan is only an eastward extension of the central one of five little chapels, and its total length would only exceed the rest by about 12 feet, and width would be a little over 11 feet.	PROVED BY EXCAVATION AS SUBSTANTIALLY CORRECT FOR THE EARLIER OR RECTILINEAR PORTION OF THE CHAPEL. The dimensions are shown in the plan published in the *Proc. Som. Arch. Soc.* for 1908, and again in 1909.

II. AS TO THE DEDICATION OF THE CHAPEL.

November 7, 1907. "**Capella St. Edgar. Abbas Beere fecit hanc capellam Beat(i) Edgar(i).** "... et capella extensit 30 virgas ... et fecit altarium ... et tumbam ante altarium gloriosam aedificavit ad memoriam Sanct(i) Edgar(i)." *Q. "Which Abbot did this?"* *A.* "**Ricardus Whitting.**"	Leland says: "Abbat Beere builded Edgares Chapel at the east end of the Church. But Abbat Whitting performed sum part of it." Willis thought that the Edgar Chapel might have been at this point—*i.e.*, where he shows his projecting central chapel.	PROVED LATER TO HAVE BEEN THE EDGAR CHAPEL BY A PLAN DISCOVERED IN 1910 IN A PRIVATE COLLECTION. (See *Som. Arch. Soc. Proc.*, 1916-17.) THE 30-YARD LENGTH IS THE RESULT OF AN ADDITION TO THE ORIGINAL PLAN.

III. AS TO A DOOR IN THE EXTREME EAST.

November 7, 1907. "**Portus introitus post reredos, post altarium quinque passuum**" (An entrance door five paces behind the reredos).

June 16, 1908. "**There was a passage to the east doore in ye walle to the streete.**"

No record of such a feature, and no warrant for supposing it. Eastern doorways are very unusual.

Nothing known of door or wall to the street from this part.

PROVED BY THE GAP FOUND IN THE FOOTINGS AT THE EASTERN EXTREMITY, WHERE THE TWO FOUNDATIONS OF THE ANGULAR APSE WALLS DO NOT JOIN. THE DEPTH OF THE APSE IS ABOUT FIVE PACES.

The use of the word "portus," meaning "door," is confirmed in this sense by the allusion to the "east door." The angular south wall of the apse continues on, and was perhaps a fence-wall to a pathway, but it has not been possible to pursue this. The ditch or moat is believed to have run on the south side of same. On the north, the footing of the angular wall stops short, leaving a gap in the foundations at the east end, as though for a doorway.

IV. AS TO THE TOTAL LENGTH OF THE CHAPEL.

November 7, 1907. "**Et capella extensit 30 virgas ad orientem**" (And the chapel extended 30 yards to the east).

The Elizabethan Inventory, in a list of measures of the Church, says: "*Chapter House, 90 feet.*" ..

PROVED BY MEASURE. THE INTERNAL MEASURE IS 87 FEET, AND THIS, ALLOWING 3 FEET MORE FOR THICKNESS OF END WALL AND PLINTH GIVES THE 30 YARDS FOR THE TOTAL LENGTH OF THE EDGAR CHAPEL.

TABLE OF THE VERIDICAL PASSAGES—*Continued.*

V. AS TO THE AZURE GLASS IN THE WINDOWS OF THE CHAPEL.

SCRIPT.	EXISTING DATA.	RESULT.
November 7, 1907. "**Et vitrea azurea**" (**And window-glass of** azure).	Azure blue does not predominate in glass of the sixteenth century. The dominant tones are white and gold, the field often being almost entirely white. The subjects are in glass of various colours. The blues tend to a steely grey.	PROVED BY THE DISCOVERY OF FRAGMENTS, RELATIVELY NUMEROUS, OF BLUE GLASS IN THE TRENCHES. THIS GLASS WAS PROBABLY REFITTED FROM THE WINDOWS OF THE EARLIER WORK ALTERED OR REMOVED BY SUCCESSIVE ABBOTS, AND APPEARS TO BE OF THE THIRTEENTH CENTURY.

VI. AS TO THE VAULTING OF "FANS."

November 7, 1907. "**Abbas Beere . . . fecit voltam petriam quod vocatur quadripartus, sed Abbas Whitting . . . destruxit . . . et restoravit eam cum nov . . . multipart . . . nescimus eam quod vocatur.** November 13, 1907. "**Wee saide that ye volte was multipartite, yt was fannes old-style in ye este ende of ye choire, and ye newe volt in Edgare's chappel Glost'er fannes.**"	It is a fair inference that a chapel of this nature and period (Henry VII. to Henry VIII.) would be vaulted in "fans," and we should have thought Abbot Bere's original scheme would have provided for this. "Fannes old style" would apply to those built on a half-hexagonal section. The real Tudor fan has a circular sweep.	THE EDGAR CHAPEL HAD THE LATER (MULTIPARTITE) FORM OF FAN, AS IS PROVED BY THE NATURE OF THE FRAGMENTS FOUND. ONE OF THE MAIN BOSSES IS EXTANT, AND ON ITS BACK HAS THE DIRECTION (IN SCORED LINES) FOR THE CORRECT SETTING OF THE BLOCK, AND THIS SHOWS TWELVE RIBS, IMPLYING A WHEEL OF TRACERY BETWEEN FANS.

VII. AS TO THE POLYGONAL EAST END.

November 19, 1907. "The direction of the walls . . . was at an angle."

November 19, 1907. "Forty and two feete was the hight of ye newe chapelle, and yt was ybuttressed with faire buttresses, and walls slantwise at ye cornere."

November 26, 1907. "The east end. Seek for the pillars, and the walls at an angle."

November 30, 1908. "The ending of the chappel was at an angle, the sides makyng as it were a baye in the east wall there."

No existing data from which such might be inferred. The nearest example of a polygonal east end seems to be at Westbury-on-Trym, near Bristol, unless we regard the Lady Chapel at Wells as a parallel instance. This chapel, however, is in reality an elongated octagon, with a domical roof. It was erected A.D. 1326.

PROVED BY DISCOVERY IN JANUARY, 1909, AFTER THE TENTATIVE PLAN OF AN ANGULAR APSE HAD BEEN IN THE PRESS FOR PUBLICATION BY THE SOMERSET ARCHÆOLOGICAL SOCIETY; AND AFTER ACTUAL PUBLICATION IN THE CHRISTMAS NUMBER OF THE *Treasury* FOR 1908.

VIII. AS TO THE DIFFERENCE IN THE FOUNDATIONS.

February 19, 1908. "Thin walls and poore foundations in the new work."

Nothing known.

PROVED BY EXCAVATION. THE FOOTING WALLS OF THE APSE WERE THIN AND POOR, IN MARKED CONTRAST TO THOSE OF THE RECTANGULAR PART OF THE CHAPEL, WHICH WERE EXCEEDINGLY BROAD.

TABLE OF THE VERIDICAL PASSAGES—*Continued.*

IX. AS TO AN OLDER LADY CHAPEL BEFORE MONINGTON'S TIME WITH A POLYGONAL APSE.

SCRIPT.	EXISTING DATA.	RESULT.
April 20, 1908. "The olde church had a chapell going east like to Edgar's, and the corners were cut off most like. The foundations ye mean remain."	Nothing known, but there is a possible inference as regards a Lady Chapel beyond the original Quire before the Western Lady Chapel was incorporated. Phelps has preserved a reminiscence of this chapel, and he suggests a semicircular end, which might mean a polygon. The projection beyond the retro-quire would be about 12 feet, according to his diagram. Compare the Lady Chapel at Wells.	IN JUNE, 1908, TRACES OF A SLANT WALL (FOOTING TRENCH) WERE FOUND CLOSE INSIDE THE EAST WALL OF THE RETRO-QUIRE AND A LITTLE SOUTH OF THE CENTRE (*recorded in a report from Rev. H. Barnwell, late Vicar of Glastonbury) written to F.B.B. shortly after the commencement of excavation.*) About 12 feet beyond the retro-quire, the levels of the ground and foundations rise considerably. At this point comes the west wall of the Edgar Chapel; and the same point probably marks the extreme eastward limit of the older Lady Chapel.
June 16, 1908. "There are two chapels, and ye must try to judge old and new. The scheme of Abbot Monington gave one, and under the church are remains yet older."	Nothing known at the time. Phelps's plan of a Lady Chapel, copied by Warner, suggests two different states of this building, the original extending under the quire, and afterwards absorbed in Monington's new work.	THE EXISTENCE OF OLDER FOOTINGS UNDER THE QUIRE FLOOR WAS PROVED LATER. THEY WERE TOO MUCH PULLED ABOUT AND ALTERED TO ESTABLISH THEIR ORIGINAL FORM.

X. AS TO THE LITTLE CRYPT UNDER THE STAIRS.

April 20, 1908. "Ye crypt was mere a chamber under the stairs, and it was at the west end of the chapel."

June 16, 1908. "The cript is fallen in, but the clay is not the old clay. Clear out the midst thereof."

Nothing known at this date of chapel, crypt, or stair. The rise of ground at east might suggest a raised floor for the chapel exterior to retro-quire. Britton's plan of Abbey suggests that the two piers found *circa* 1813 on the site of the middle chapel of the retro-quire were " probably part of a crypt," but there was nothing known to warrant such a suggestion, and facts were against it.

THE NECESSITY OF A STAIRCASE TO BERE'S CHAPEL IS PROVED BY THE SUBSEQUENT DISCOVERY OF ITS SUPERIOR LEVEL—PROBABLY SOME SEVEN FEET ABOVE THE RETRO-QUIRE. AS THE GROUND RISES IMMEDIATELY EAST OF THE WEST WALL OF THE CHAPEL, IT ALMOST INEVITABLY FOLLOWS THAT A CRYPT WOULD BE CONFINED TO A SMALL SPACE BENEATH THE ANTECHAPEL OR STAIRWAY OF APPROACH.

XI. AS TO THE DOUBLE HAND-RAIL.

"And ye stairway was divided in ye midst by a grete rail of stone," etc.

Nothing known at the time.

A DOUBLE-HANDED STONE RAIL WAS DETECTED LATER AMONG THE DÉBRIS LYING ABOUT THE ABBEY QUIRE WALLS NOT FAR FROM THE SITE OF THE CHAPEL.

TABLE OF THE VERIDICAL PASSAGES—*Continued.*

XII. AS TO THE WIDTH OF BERE'S BUILDING.

SCRIPT.	EXISTING DATA.	RESULT.
June 16, 1908. "The width ye shall find is twenty and seven, and outside thirty and four, so we remember.—BEERE, Abbas."	Nothing known.	THE WEST WALL OF THE CHAPEL MEASURES ABOUT 31 FEET 6 INCHES. 27 FEET IS A PROBABLE MEASURE FOR THE INTERIOR WIDTH OF THE CHAPEL, WHOSE WALLS, DEEPLY RECESSED FOR THE WINDOWS, WOULD STAND WELL UPON THE OUTER PART OF THE FOOTINGS. THESE ARE 6 FEET 6 INCHES WIDE ON THE NORTH AND SOUTH. THE OUTER, OR 32 FEET MEASURE DOES NOT INCLUDE THE BUTTRESSES.

XIII. AS TO THE LENGTH OF BERE'S BUILDING.

SCRIPT.	EXISTING DATA.	RESULT.
June 16, 1908. "Wee laid down seventy and two, but they builded longer."	Nothing known or recorded. No inference possible.	PROVED AS A MEASURE SUBSTANTIALLY CORRECT FOR THE SUPERSTRUCTURE, AS INFERRED FROM THE FOOTINGS. (See plans in *Som. Arch. Soc. Proc.* for 1908-9.)

	ft. in.
Antechapel .. (approx.)	12 0
Bere's Rectangular Chapel (5 + 50 + 5)	60 0
	72 0

XIV. AS TO A CEILING IN GOLD AND CRIMSON.

June 16, 1908). "And he who followed made new schemes for a certaine roofe in golde and crimson."

Nothing known or recorded.

PROVED BY THE SUBSEQUENT DISCOVERY OF ARCH-MOULDINGS WITH MEMBERS PAINTED IN RED AND BLACK, AND RETAINING TRACES OF GOLD.

XV. AS TO A CHAPEL OF FOUR BAYS.

February 19, 1908. "And the chamber was in length 70 feet, in four bays."

Nothing known and no inference possible.

THE RECTANGULAR CHAPEL PROVED TO BE OF FOUR BAYS. THE 70 FEET INCLUDES THE ANTECHAPEL, BUT IS A ROUND-FIGURE ESTIMATE, THE TRUE LENGTH BEING ABOUT 72. (See XIII. above.)

XVI. AS TO THE ALTAR SCREEN AND TRIPLE ARCADE.

December 2, 1908. "The procession path went round three corners, and they builded the new window after hys time straight. Ye have found the old wall before Monington, I guess, but do not know.... Hee (Monington) did make the Est end full square, that I know he didd, and in hym three arches and a grete screene."

Nothing known at the time. At Wells there are three arches between quire and retro-quire, behind the reredos, and a similar arrangement at Glastonbury would easily be inferred.

THE EXCAVATION PROVED THAT THERE WERE FORMERLY THREE ARCHES BEHIND THE ALTAR, AND THERE WERE INDICATIONS OF A SCREEN WALL BETWEEN.

ADDENDUM TO THE TABLE OF THE VERIDICAL PASSAGES.

Script.	Existing Data.	Result.
December 2, 1908. "Soe it was in my day, that he who followed after did enlong the window, and it was full weake and they rebuilded it. He did build strong walls over ye lytell chapel of Our Ladye that then was, and in them a new window, and on either side he placed a walle which did continue the walls of the choire, and did put in an arche and under hym a tombe on either side with the altar in the midst, and above the arche as it was two grete high windows very narrow, which did make on to the grete east window, and wyth hym made a grete faire window which did light up all the choir," etc.	The suggestion is that one of the Abbots coming after Monington substituted for his square east and a bayed end with a principal window flanked by two narrow ones set anglewise. The great east window of Glo'ster is slightly bayed and has buttressings for support to the east. It is recorded that in Bere's day the great east window was " casting out", and had to be given further support.	Nothing can be proved as regards any later alteration of the east window, as all above ground is cleared away.

EXTRACT FROM LETTER OF HON. EVERARD
FEILDING, SECRETARY OF THE SOCIETY FOR
PSYCHIC RESEARCH, TO THE AUTHOR, DATED
15th MARCH, 1917.

" MY DEAR BOND,

" . . . As to your record of the script, it
would be most interesting if you were to publish
it. There is no question but that the writing
about the Edgar Chapel preceded the discovery
of it by many months. I was present, if you remember, at what I believe was the beginning of
the recrudescence of ——'s automatism, . . .
and that was before you ever started your work
at Glastonbury, and before you were even appointed to the work. I remember your telling
me when you were appointed, how interesting it
was, as you were then able to test some of the
statements made.

" No, there is no doubt whatever in my mind
on that point; you will remember that the only
doubt I have ever expressed was on the question
as to how far something in one of the books on
Glastonbury which you showed me afterwards,
and which might have suggested the possibility
of the actual position of the Edgar Chapel, might
conceivably have influenced ——'s mind sub-
consciously; I forget what book it was, but I remember it was not the book which was taken at
that time as the most authoritative."

Signed Statement of J.A.

" I, the undersigned J—— A——, hereby certify that I am the J.A. referred to in Mr. Bligh Bond's account of the automatic writings concerning Glastonbury Abbey and other matters, and that the transcript which he has made of the series of about fifty communications dating from 7th November, 1907, to 30th November, 1911, and also some supplementary writings produced in 1912 and later, appears to me correct so far as the same could be deciphered by us. I furthermore affirm that the writings were produced through my hand, but without knowledge of their nature or purport, and contain conclusions which I could not have arrived at normally, and which in many cases—as, *e.g.*, in the case of the Edgar Chapel—were such as appeared to me most improbable, and were deemed fanciful until further research had elucidated points then obscure. My knowledge and reading were confined to documents which have been accessible to all students of the Abbey, and I had no unique source of information. The writings were produced often whilst my normal attention was devoted to other matters, and promiscuous conversation at these times was our rule. I held the pencil and Mr. Bond laid his fingers on the back of my hand or lightly grasped it. He did not direct it. There was nothing in my knowledge or experience that I know of to suggest the names of Bryant and

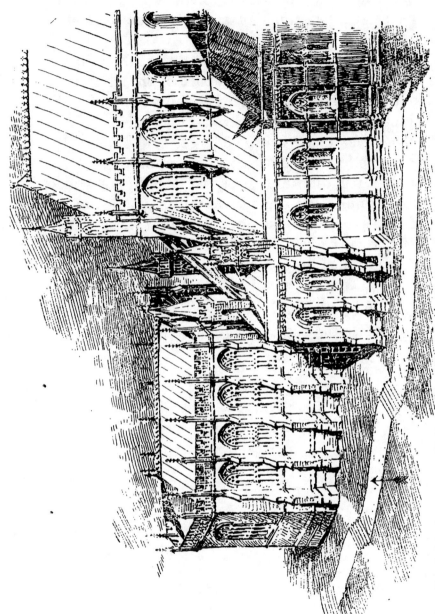

Fig. 8.—Conjectural Appearance of the East End of the Abbey in the Sixteenth Century, showing the Edgar Chapel on Left Hand, the Retro-Quire and Monington's Addition of Two Bays to the Quire, all as viewed from the North Side.

The arrow indicates the position of a conjectural north chantry (see text).

6

others which are appended to the writings.   Even the possible meaning of such a name as Manu-metaxyl was unknown to me.[1]

" I am disposed to concur with Mr. Bond in the view that the subconscious part of the mind may in its operation traverse the limitations of individual knowledge, either acting telepathically through contact with some larger field of memory, or as itself part of a larger unit of a more pervasive kind as regards time and space, conditions which would imply that the individual may have powers of self-expression far greater than those which are normally available through the brain-mechanism controlled by the will and logical faculties.

" GLOUCESTER,
    "*July 24th*, 1917."

[1] This refers to a portion of the script not yet published.

PART II

THE CHILD OF NATURE

LINES ON A PICTURE OF RESTORED GLASTONBURY.

Short-sighted Reason pondered long alone;
   Experience and Deduction lent their aid;
They measured well and carefully each stone,
   And calculated where each groin was laid;
But still th' elusive vision of the Past
Evaded each attempt to hold it fast !

Then came Imagination, Maid Divine,
   And forthwith, wakened from its resting-place,
The Past arose, till pictured line on line
   The Abbey stood in all its ancient grace.
Awestruck, they gazed upon that House of Prayer,
Then silently went in, and worshipped there.

Thus, in the places waste and desolate,
   Where saintly spirits struggled through the night,
In ages past, you still may find the Gate
   Of Heaven open, letting down the light;
Still find on Yniswitrin's altars, pale,
The gleaming vision of the Holy Grail.

JOHN ALLEYNE.

1917.

PLATE III.

GLASTONBURY ABBEY.

Conjectural reconstruction of interior (drawn in 1908) as seen from the north transept, looking towards the Quire. N.B.—The arch in the foreground, communicating with a supposed western aisle, is an artistic license.

Frontispiece to Part II.

THE CHILD OF NATURE

JOHANNES—who is he ? The child of our dreams ? Or a name inscribed in the great roll of those who were, and now are not ?

No previous knowledge of surname or circumstance, either in history or fiction, can be traced as a source of the idea underlying this dramatisation of a personality in many respects so sympathetic and so true to nature.

Yet again and again he speaks, or is spoken for, in the writings, and his simplicity of character is maintained. And he became to us more than a name, one vested with reality, even as it is said of a well-known author, that his characterisations dwelt in his consciousness as living folk. And we never knew when his advent might be expected, nor what sort of message he would have for us. Frequently it happened that in sitting down to writing some expectation or desire would be expressed for information on certain lines, but the script would negative this expectation, and either give us something new and quite unexpected, or else, as often happened, take up the thread of a previous communication broken off several days, or even months before.

" . . . He ever loved the woods and the pleasant places which lie without our house. It was good, for he learnt in the temple of nature much that he would never hear in choro. His herte was of the country and he heard it calling without the walls and the Abbot winked at it for he knew full well that it was good for him. He went a-fishing, did Johannes, and tarried oft in lanes to listen to the birds and to watch the shadows lengthening over all the woods of Mere.

" He loved them well, and many times no fish had he, for that he had forgot them . . . but we cared not, for he came with talk and pleasant converse, as nutbrown ale, and it was well.

" And because he was of nature his soul was pure and he is of the Company that doth watch and wait for the glories to be renewed."

It was in the fourth sitting that Johannes, instead of being the spokesman, was spoken for.

" Gulielmus de Glaston shall speke . . . hath spoken of his tyme, and Johannes wold speke of hys time. The older tyme wasne known to hym. My punishment is past, but Johannes is yet in pain."

SITTING XI. 4th January, 1908.

At this sitting Johannes speaks for another, as follows:

" . . . wold say, ' Seek ye goal and ensue it. Ne walke in circles as somme doe. Many objects distract ye minde. Seeke one goal and wynne all.
" JOHANNES DE GLASTON."

In response to a question about two friends:

" Dreme. To them is to dreme, not labour. Seek visions. Be constant in mind.

" That wych cometh, doe. Wee may not say more. To you is to choose. Opus spiriti, non opus terrae est. Ye are rich, but not in goodes. Work at that which comes."

SITTING XVIII. 18th February, 1908.

" Stande ye, and be as waxe in oure hands. Listen, and ye shall heare. I, Johannes, say soe. Be patient and yielding. Listen for our voices in choro mid. Ye shall heare them, and much more, but persevere : great things shall come to pass ere ye join the Company. Goe ye and prosper for us and you. Wee waite where wee wold bee.

" JOHANNES."

SITTING XXVI. 12th March, 1908.

This communication bears the names of others besides Johannes, but is included owing to its interesting nature.

" The horloge as ye face the wall lieth on the right, six elles or more above the floor. The stair in the right towret led from ye cloister to it, to wind hym every day at matins.

" I, Galfrith, knew in my day. They who came spake in Latin, and not all knew the wisdom hid in the british tongue, nor eke the saxon. Some were wrote again, but the fathers were more sought than the Bards and much was hearsay.

" What do ye long after, my son ? The memory of man is but as the grass that fadeth, and they who would fain translate the word of the barbarian oft inserted what they desired but would not an they could (? *translate truly*). The hidden meaning they knew not which looked for the husk which covered it and soe much was lost for all tyme. The merlins spoke in what ye call an allegory, but the parable was what these fathers read, not the mystery.

" Those who would tell you of the glory of our howse all strive together, Saxon, Norman, and native, so which wold ye have—Norman base or later Abbey ?

" Ye see the howse in its first condition, and like a falling lace, the dremes of later men obscure it. The first dreme improved—it was complete, and the grete church as it stood when Jocelyn came is what ye wish,

" Then, when they were building at Welles, we were jealous of our howse, and certain masons coming on holiday across the causeway which led straight across the marsh, did tell us we were lacking. They sedde our howse was over smalle for our community, and the choir thereof was not long enow for our processions and for the brethren to sitte at the service of the church—for we were three hundred and forty-seven in number. And moreover the towre was too lowe for beauty. And Wells being new and faire with carven stone, our Abbot was moved to beautify our howse. Soe he that was at enmity with Jocelyn, made friends that day, and the Bishop with a fair company came on a white palfrey and did dine with us. And so was our choir enlonged and afterwards the towre was beautifyed with certain panelling, and this although our coffers were much in need because the body of the church was newly yfinished by very faire art.

" Ye belle Towre that was burnt and new builded was pulled downe because it was falling (on) ye cloister, for it was sunken in the foote."

The above being far from clearly written, a repetition of the last sentences was asked for.

" Nay, my sonne. Have I not told ? And ye would know of ye belle-towre. It was not. I have sedde it was pulled downe and ne heard of. The gabell was yfinished like unto Welles, and the clock and certain belles did hang there.

"ONE OF THE COMPANY.

" *My name* JOHANNES GLASTON.

" *Ego Frater* PETRUS LIGHTFOTE
    (*qui horologium deditet dedicavit*)."

SITTING XXXVII. 23rd September, 1908.

" We have sat in the grate gallery under the west window and watched the pylgrims when the sun went downe. It was in truth a brave sight, and one to move the soul of one there. The orgayne that did stande in the gallery did answer hym that spake on the great screene, and men were amazed not knowing which did answer which. Then did ye bellows blowe and ye . . . man who beat with his hands upon the manual did strike yet harder, and all did shout Te Deums, so that all ye town heard the noise of the shouting, and ye little orgaynes in ye chapels did join in the triumph. Then ye belles did ring and we thought hyt must have gone to ye gates of Heaven. But we know not now, for there were sinnes, and the frailties and pomps of men are not meet for the ear of Hym that dwelleth in the heavens."

(Here follows a reference to a certain Radulphus, whose story had been previously given.)

"More we will serche in the great army of past things— they are soe hard to find."

SITTING XL. 15th October, 1909 (shortly after the excavation of the corner of the vault beneath the refectory)

". . . He fell full sore and lay as one dead, and the King was right merrie. 'See,' he said, 'how heavy lies the good ale on this poor roysterer.'

"And my Abbot did make penances full sore and many, so that Johannes had need of drink and good cheere to help his weakness. '(O) for the full bowle,' quoth he, '. . . for one good drink; there is so much amiss.'

"And ye have found the place wherein I lay, and even now the scent of good ale hangs round the floores. I go, who have told ye. Peccavi!'

"'Well,' saith Father Abbot, 'ye have disgraced us before ye Kinge, and he will not remember us in the day of our adversity.'

"'Nay,' saith Johannes, 'but the Kinge, who was of an evil choler, was afterwards right merrie because of poor Johannes and the vat of good ale. Alas! That soe much of good ale was squandered for a King's pastime!' Whereat there went more Paternosters and much penance in claustro. Ye have it. What more wold ye?"

The foregoing was very difficult to decipher, and its substance so entirely different from anything we might have expected, that practically nothing could at the time be made of it. It was therefore asked for again.

"I have told ye. Why ask me more? They who brought the vat of ale pulled hym uppe with a rope, for ye King called for more brown ale such as we in ye Abbey were wont to brew. Ye rope broke, and ye King was merrie, and this I say, gainsay who may, it was not Johannes and ye ale which destroyed our faire Abbey, but ye lust of ye King and ye haste which (he had for the possession) of our house.

"Why did they say that I who soe loved my Abbey, had compassed its ruin? I didde paternosters for that which wasne my sinne. Ye rope it broke. Hee was the misdoer.

"Ye Guesten Hall was over against the Monks' Hall, and there were, as you say, great screenen between the two tables, and ye Abbate hadde his high table, and likewise ye Kinge had his, but they had an screne. The Kinge's party did royster in their cuppes.

"What of ye Hall? Faire tapestry and carven oake, and six high windowes in the syde of him, and one faire windowe in ye gables, and under hym a gallery where were singing men to please the King's majestie, and cunning minstrelsie. Ye pulpitte was silent—not homilies, but the brethren did list to songs of prowess and pleasure instead of paternosters. But in that pollution was death to our howse, for the Kinge did lust after our meats and wines and (cared) not to save us from (the coming doom); and he whom we trusted, the great Cardinal, was falling, although we knew it not. 'Wait,' said our Abbot, 'he is our friend who made me Abbot. Ask hym to our house.'"

This passage was again very difficult to decipher, and before anything had been made of it I asked for it again. J.A. was without any idea of its contents.

" I did say there were windowes six in ye grete Halle, and a grete one at the gables, wherein were singing mennes. I didde sayye that the Kinge lusted after our Howse and (was covetous) of our good cheere, fit for a Kinge's majestie. This proved the ruin of our howse, for hee who made our Abbot was himself falling from greatness, and could give us no help—hee, the Cardinal of Ipswich.

" But ne'er was it Johannes and ye ale!"

SITTING XLII. 18th April, 1911.

The foundations of the chapel of St. Dunstan at the west end of the Lady Chapel had been brought to light, and were evidently of mixed date—the original probably very early.

Q. by F.B.B. " Who built St. Dunstan's Chapel ?"

" Edgarus ybuilded long syne. Radulphus hoc opus restoravit. After hym ye fyre yburned yt. Then he was a capella in muro.[1]

" They say we hadde not hys bonen, but they lie, for we hadde the leg-bones of hym, and certain smalle bones which they took to Canterbury, and Johannes knoweth it of old tyme long syne. They did open the tombe and tooke them backe. What mean they who said we hadde them not ? They all knew it, and the pilgrimmes did come from Canterbury by ye old horse-way to venerate them.

" Roof yfallen! Hee of the gatehouse dwelt therein, and it wasne Capella—vae mihi! Went! Ye King commanded! Because we all who should obey were meek. And soe it was not.

" JOHANNES DE GLASTON."

SITTING XLIX. 29th July, 1911.

This little fragment came quite spontaneously and without anything to lead up to it.

[1] The remains lie on the line of the wall (now removed) which divide l the Inner from the Outer Bailey.

"At night the sound of many waters refreshed ye parched soil. From tower and from the high roofes the sound came like the sound of waterfloods, and the gargoyles shouted each to each, and the cloisters whispered comfort and refreshment as we lay under the dormer roofe in parched and sultry nights.

"I who speak mind me of the glory of sound even now, and I ever loved the waters and the mere, and the voices that whispered around me. Therefore went I a-fishing on the mere, and the glories of nature were yet more glorious than the Te Deums in choro. Therefore loved I the rain on our hundred roofs, and the myriad voices that came from the waterspouts.

"I didde sleepe on the south side, hard by the great gabell, and soe heard I the sound whilst others slept. Vai mihi, that it is departed! and the voices are heard no more."

SITTING L.   30th July, 1911.

Although neither of us was aware of the fact, this sitting was destined to be the last of the series. Except for a few occasions in 1912, it proved impossible to continue these experiments. But Sitting XLIX. ends with a message of farewell, and so, it will be seen, does the last of the series. And in some respects the substance of the writing is a sort of review of the part played by Johannes, and offers an explanation of the related influences which is full of interesting suggestion.

"Simple he was, but as a dog loveth his master, so loved he his Howse with a greater love than any of them that planned and builded it. They were of the earth—planners and builders for their great glory, nor ever, though honest men, for the glory of God. But Johannes, mystified and bewildered by its beauty, gave it his heart, as one gives his heart to a beloved mistress; and so, being earthbound by that love, his spirit clings in dreams to the vanished vision which his spirit-eyes even still see.

" Even as of old he wandered by the mere and saw the sunset shining on her far-off towers, and now in dreams the earth-love part of him strives to picture the vanished glories, and led by the masonry of love, he knows that ye also love what he has loved, and so he strives to give you glimpses of his dreams.

" Simple child of Nature—loving her, he knew not why ; but loving her yet more deeply because he knew not why he loved. He was not meant to be a priest of the choire, and it harassed him sometimes overmuch. Child of Nature! He loved freedom, and was happier in the orchard, and by the mere, than performing the rituals of the choir.

" Men loved him for his love, but ofttimes his Prior comprehended not, and mistaking the outward show in which he failed, for lack of that inner worship which they could not feel, they made him do penances for which their backs were more fitted. Then ye should know who would understand him aright, and read his inner meaning.

" He would tell you what he saw, but how can he describe it ? It was beautiful, and his soul rejoiced as he would have you also rejoice, but he could not tell you why. It was good. It was pleasing to the eye, and through the eye his soul was uplifted, in an age when souls were grovelling.

" It was lovely, and he knew it, but when ye ask, ' What was it like unto?' he cannot tell you. It was heavenly—so was the sunset—and the shadows on the mere—but he could not paint these nor reproduce them for you.

" Those others, the great and simple, are passed and gone to other fields, and they remember not save when the love of Johannes compels their mind to some memory before forgotten.

" Then through his soul do they dimly speak, and Johannes, who understands not, is the link that binds you to them.

" Learn and understand.

" WE WHO ARE THE WATCHERS.

" Farewell."

SITTING LI.   (First of new series.)   26th January,
1912.

No previous questions asked.

"HÆREWITH the Dane hath learned the greater
wisdom.   Many gods there be, but though many names,
the principles are but two—Good and Evil, Love and Hate.
Therefore, when he slew the Saxons, he knew not that he
followed Evil, but repenting long since, he hath embraced
Love, which is Good, and his task is easy.   Therefore is
he of the brotherhood, working with a glad heart to
expiate for ever the evil he once did, and therefore in
constant labour there in the joy of Heaven.

" 'Purgatorio' would some of the brethren say, but the
Purgatorio is Paradise, if the intent be perfect and the
suffering has no half-heartedness.   For awhile there is
joy in sins, but only till the day cometh.   Run the race
with a whole heart, not as the lukewarm ones.   Happiness
is in the extremes, but the only joy which lasts for ever
and grows for ever is the joy of striving for the Good.

" Thus was it of the beneficial influence of Glastonbury."

" Hærewith the Dane hath spoken—once warrior, now
striving ever for the good.   Be not faint-hearted; strive
your utmost—therein lies happiness.   Labour, and even
suffering, make Paradise, not Purgatorio.   Thus have I
spoken."

(Influence changes.)

" Up cometh Johannes, weake by reason of long syne.
What wold ye ?   Ye have founden our Church, and ye
holy places where my unworthy feet have trod, and the
Hall where some did talk of Glaston and some did eat
that they might be strong for God's ordinances.   And ye
have found ye lytell chapple where our most holy ones did
lie.   Enow, what think ye ?

" Ye walle with the postern, and ye courtyard over
against the graveyard and the antechamber cometh, and
beyond hym the Grete Chambre wherein the folk did
gather upon the feasts.   Then cometh the grete Kitchen
and over agaynst (hym) the well-chamber in the courtyard

is ygone, but ye well is there, but yfilled.   Certain rude men
did go down hym to find ye Treasure, but found yt not,
tho' they drew off the water nigh twenty cubits.   Then
cast they in the walls and filled him up because Johannes
Parsons the cowherd fell in and was slayn, whereat they
said, ' The spirit of our Abbot is abroad and hath ytaken
vengeance.'

"Then ycometh the grete Kyng's Gate into ye inner
courtyarde wherein were no trees but only a grete passage-
way of paving.

"And he was high of roofe, nigh forty feet, yvaulted,
and over hym a chamber, and ye door in ye side dydde leade
to apartments for the laity.   And soe to the Kitchen court,
but ye almoner John Bryan dydde live over the grete gate
and a porter did dwell at his call on ye south side.   There
too was a turret and a grete bell the which was ringed for
the meals in the King's Chambre.   But he is all gone long
syne—heu mihi!"

*   *   *   *   *

"I dydde it not, God wot, not I!   Why cling I to that
which is not ?   It is I, and it is not I, butt parte of me
which dwelleth in the past and is bound to that whych my
carnal soul loved and called ' home ' these many years.
Yet I, Johannes, amm of many partes, and ye better parte
doeth other things—Laus, Laus Deo!—only that part
which remembreth clingeth like memory to what it seeth
yet."

SITTING LIV. 17th August, 1912.

"Johannes now very far away : far, in that the force is
weake : even soe may be within you and yet farre away, for
the strength is as the distance ; the one changeth as
the other.   Wee wold saye much, but the weakness here
is strength gathered for other duties.   All, he cannot
do.   What wold ye ? . . . The stones written in his
memory as he knew them ?   What are real, and what
are in his dreme, he knows not.[1] . . .   It cease(th) . . .
and yet it remayneth in him ever the same.   What wold
he tell you ?—cannot read your wishes."

[1] A possible source of error in the communications, which may
describe occasionally as still existing, things which have perhaps
been rooted out by vandals of modern date.

" Digged ye—what dig ye for by the towre of the stair-way to the lodgings of the laymen where of late they put those who were sick ?   From ye passage and stayre that leadeth from ye Cloyster to the old Kirkeyarde open to hym, and there was a doore in ye passage way and a staire four-square. Yt opened to the lay-housen. On the floor the lay-chamber for foregathering and above hym the dormitory and lytell chambere above, with doores from ye stayre to each and on ye south side a doore down to the Refectorium misericorde, and one into the gallery under ye window that looketh west, and the courtyarde of flagged stone and the Guesten Hall. So yt was. And the passage way of our Lord Abbot opened from ye wall to ye yarde from ye Abbot's covered walk yvaulted in stone."

SITTING LXI.   9th December, 1912.

In answer to a question:

" This have I told ye. I slept beneath the roof where lay those (who) were fleshy and weighty. So it was ordained that we should doe.

" Soe I remember those stayres for my fatness. But it availed me not, tho' my father Prior recommended it oft. Alas! I waxed more fat.

" Not that my belly was my god. I wot not! But I was cheery and troubled not, save for services in ecclesia, for better loved I the lanes and the woods where walked I much—with weariness because of my weight.

" So said I, ' It is the Lord's will. Somme be made fat, and somme be lean '; and this I said to they that jibed, that the gates of Heaven are made full wide for all sorts, so that none created should stick within the portall. This I said, for they vexed me with their quips.

" I would remind me of many things. Half do I re-member—yet the lytell things only. The greate ones (stick) even as I myself stuck in the portal by reason of their trick, and Johannes, as once before, cannot rayse themme and lies beneath their weight. I wold explain but must gaine strength. . . .

" I was ever soe : of a merry heart, when like to melte

in tears. So was I made. It was not my fault. Light of thought, save the thoughts I could not speak ; and the light jests comme again to me. Glad soule! Had I but turned my soul to the things that were greate, I should not be now a child among the toys. But I was never meant to be a monk. They placed me here in choro, when I would have drawn the sword. . . .''

EXTRACT FROM SCRIPT OBTAINED 15TH SEPTEMBER, 1912.

" But one waiteth, even Johannes, whose body, scattered to the winds of Heaven, once lay in the cemetery of the monks, hard by the east side of the Chapel of St. Michael in the midst of the graveyard. What matter ? He lives yet in the universal Memory, and speaks and acts through every channel in which the Universal Life flows.

" Yet when he is himself, he speaks well, as he was wont in the rude times that are as yesterday."

In these brief yet pregnant passages the author's philosophy is brought to a focus. Humbling the arrogance of the individual mind, because it denies that the mere mechanism of the human brain can ever *originate* idea, it yet raises the little limited self to the consciousness of a possibility, awful and beautiful, of a contact with something greater than itself, and yet akin; and to the dignity of a mystical fellowship in which isolation ends, and Past and Present are seen as parts of a living whole; points in the circumference of a circle whose radius is Life beyond these limitations. Our little mechanism we may attune to respond to the needs, the pleasures, and the interests of our own fragmentary span; or, disdaining these, we may harmonise it to the thought which is pictured on the great outward sweep of the circle

7

of Memory, recorded there by the lives of those of far distant times. Then will these records live again for us and through the gates of our soul will pour, from the living source of Idea, their ordered recollections. Not by our own power, but through the unseen Gate of the subconscious mind, will these memories link themselves with ours—not through the evocation of the "spirit" of Johannes, but by the power of the Universal Spirit, whose life permeates all the regions of Time, and in Whom we and Johannes, and all who are in mental kinship with his thought, are as one.

THE GARGOYLE.

In mid-June, 1908, whilst the work of excavation was still in its preliminary stage, J.A. and F.B.B. were both at Glastonbury. At the western end of the little town, at a fork in the road, stands the lesser of the two surviving mediæval churches, that which is locally known as St. Benedict's, but which is in reality dedicated to Benignus, a companion of St. Patrick when he came to Glastonbury in the fifth century. This church was erected on the site of a much older chapel, by Abbot Richard Bere, whose arms and initials appear over the north porch. It has a fine western tower of the regular Somerset type, and on the cornice of the belfry are several carved gargoyles, the most prominent position, in the centre of the west side, being occupied by a piece of carving which, when seen from the west, as one approaches the town, has the appearance of a well-executed head of an Abbot,

with a tall jewelled mitre and lappets. The face
is bold, and full of character, rather long, with
level brows and austere expression.

From the narrowness of the road, on nearer
approach, a side view of the carving can only be
obtained by turning the head up at a somewhat
uncomfortable angle; and probably for this
reason the extraordinary fact had apparently
quite escaped attention that this was in reality

FIG. 9.

no human head at all, but a peculiar grotesque
animal, with extended neck, crouching against the
wall in a manner peculiar to gargoyles, and with
a high arched back like a fighting cat, garnished
with knobbly vertebræ. It was J.A. who first
noticed this, and called F.B.B.'s attention to it.
Both were naturally much interested, though, of
course, it was the excavation work at the Abbey
which was the chief object of attention at the time,

and this was quite a side-issue. Shortly afterwards a sitting was held, and the following is the record:

SITTING XXXII. 16th June, 1908.

Q. by F.B.B. "With reference to the sculptured boss on Saint Benedict's tower, which from different points of view appears as an Abbot's head and as a grotesque animal: was this intended for a joke ?"

A. "Wee know not the quips of they who worked for us and did sometimes bee rude to them in powers. We builded Benedicts. Wee know not what they wrought soe only the church was faire and sound for ye people. The greate workmen and ye masons of repute played noe such pranks in our Abbey church, we wot.

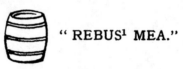 " REBUS[1] MEA."

SITTING XXXIII. 17th June, 1908.

" I, Johannes Lory, Master mason of ye Guild of St. Andrew, carving of ye gargoyle of St. Benedick, came downe from my laddere and walked, for it was colde and in Octobere. Then turning backe I saw my worke was like unto our Abbot, and soe I carved anew and made it proper. Of a truth it was our Abbot, and soe sayd they who looked. It was not my intent, but soe it was, and methinks our goode master ye Abbot knew not. Of a veritie it was most like, and soe wee left it.

" Seek it of a morning when the sun shines not ; ye shal see the more truthfully. I meant no despyte, God wot."

[1] *I.e.*, the Abbot's "rebus" (F.B.B.). A *rebus* is the enigmatic equivalent of a name. Many of these are known to have been adopted by Bishops and other ecclesiastics of note. In the case of Bere, the significance is obvious. Where a name ended in " ton," as Morton, Pereton, etc., a " tun," or barrel, has been used to complete the rebus.

SCRIPT OBTAINED AT OXFORD.   F.B.B. AND
J.A. (Present, B. Blackwell and Miss D.
Sayers.)   25th August, 1917.

No previous questions.   After a short passage
in Latin, which cannot be deciphered:

" Wolsey the Cardinal housing me with the King, and
did appoint me Abbot, olde man that I was.

" Here was the Hall that he builded in this town in
Chancellorium.

" I have said I came to Oxford, and Wolsey the Cardinal
did make me Lord Abbot in ye Hall that he had builded.
I was old and infirm, and came not on my palfrey, but
they carried me on my litter, and soe I, the old man, did
become Abbot in mine old age.   Would God I had not
been so ; then had my death been otherwise.

" Know ye the Hall which he ybuilded ?   It was where
ye now lie.

" I came not on ye palfrey.   At ye Abbey of Westminster I lay a long tyme, for I was sick.   And with ye
Cardinal came I to Oxford, and he made me Abbot, I not
willing.   I sleeped at Westminster.   There saw I the King
and would know why he desired me for a friend, I being
Treasurer of mine Abbey.   And soe yt was to be."

The day before this sitting (Friday, 24th August)
I was in the Bodleian during the morning, and
looked at Dugdale's *Monasticon*, from which I
made the following extract: "On Beere's death,
47 monks devolved the election of their Abbot to
Cardinal Wolsey, who declared Richard Whiting,
then Chancellor of the House, their Abbot." I
had not shown this to J.A., nor had there been any
reference to Whiting in our conversation. The
reference to this episode in the script obtained on
the following day would therefore seem to involve
an element of pure mental telepathy, of an entirely

subconscious nature since the matter was not in my thoughts at the time of the sitting.—F.B.B.

SITTING XVA. 1st February, 1908

This record has not been included in the general series, as the subject-matter proved to be quite foreign to anything hitherto appearing, or having reference to Glastonbury. It is given as a specimen of the "intrusions" which from time to time broke the continuity of the main subject of the writings.

First, a spiral coil was drawn, followed by some letters or characters not possible to decipher. Next a lozenge or rectangle; then a larger oblong surmounted by a semicircle, as if to indicate a domed building, a ramped line running at an angle therefrom; and finally, a cross. Then the following:

"IBERICUS, who wandered hither bringing strange gifts and treasure. Watch ye, for out of the wish it is created, and out of the myth will come the solid truth. Mystery of Faith and of Matter! Out of a thought all things were created, and out of a thought will old-time things renew their being.

"ONE OF THE CONTROLLERS
"OF THINGS THAT ARE.
"A THOUGHT IN BEING."

Next followed more vague pencillings, and several lines of quite undecipherable script, the only two words legible being CONSTANTINUS and JUSTINIAN. The writing clears up towards the end of the page, and proceeds thus:

"... who followed the Phoenician keels to far-off Isles of the Sea whose treasure was great; whom Phaedrus took in his ship to seek for safety and merchandise in one. Phaedrus gained much tin, and left him on these shores, a Prince among them, marrying Yseuguilt their Princess, and they the forebears of a royal line. (Of) the countries of the Iberi and Kymri they sat upon the thrones, and gave the world the Name that lives in all the nations.

"Who am I? One that sojourned with them from Capernaum through the Isles of Greece and past the straits which Pharos lighted to stormy seas and black rocks where the metals be.

"North, the settlement Tintagella; south, the river mouths, and inland to the forest-lands and the marshes where the rising of the sun. There builded he a Temple such as was of old in Judah, and there he reigned. Thus was I, O man! my name Phocis the Mariner."

In tracing on a map of Cornwall the course indicated in the script, east from the coast between Tintagel and Padstow, my finger lighted on a village on the fringe of Bodmin moor, marked "Temple." Neither I nor J.A. were conscious of the existence of this place-name, nor could we recall our attention having been at any time directed to it.

As to the identity of the royal traveller, the script does not yield a definite statement. If the name is there, it is to be feared that it is irrecoverable owing to the hopelessly obscure nature of the writing in the undeciphered portion. He came from Capernaum, and he came—or was it Phædrus?—seeking for safety and merchandise in one. Can we identify his Princess? Yseuguilt, or Yseult, is one perhaps of many, but it may be that some record is yet extant of a Cornish Yseult who married an Eastern prince or merchant.

And what have the antiquaries to say of Temple?
Whence did this little place derive its interesting name? Was it merely from a house of the
fraternity of the Templars, or from some far older
and now half-mythical tradition, lost in the
mists of antiquity?

In a script dated 24 April, 1918, the following
passage occurs:

"The flow of spiritual forces is westward, following and impelling
the forces of material things. By a law of revolution or rotation from
all points in the spiritual universe, this movement is universal. This
being so, the material things first appear, working on a motive very
often in itself most mundane and from your point of view most unspiritual.
Thus they whose habitation was in Crete, revisiting the memories and
traditions of the same race and civilisation which long before had been
impelled westward beyond the great continents of America to the shores
of Asia, and thence onwards through the desolate tracts of Asia to the
great Mediterranean basin, still continued the interminable route ever
westward beyond the gates of Hercules to the islands where the fire-
drawn metals be: so, as mundane influences impelled them, great immigration was induced by the want of metals for the embellishment of
temples, the discovery of bronze for warlike purposes and, in short, for
the many needs of man's development in civilisation and knowledge.
But soon the spiritual forces which developed and sustained this immigration had deeper objects in view. They followed and transformed it
by removing mundane influences, and a great spiritual development
arose in the places in which their instruments had prepared the soil,
Phocis of the race of Crete trading with Poseidon and seeking its
treasure. Powerful was their thought in contact with them who
worshipped the One God in contradistinction to the many. . . . This
paved the way for the building of a Temple in his settlement of Tintagella. . . . Thus first arose that measurement and design which were
afterwards as accurately reproduced by that further advance which
culminated in the temple of Glastonbury. . . .

"And Tintagella was the ancient place of the shrine of the High God.
So the Temple, a reproduction, accurate in every measurement was
reproduced at Glaston on this foundation. . . .

"Phocis was Phocis—a centre and nucleus, a force rightly named but
in himself but a merchant prince of Poseidon and Eubeia."[1]

[1] This seems written in defence of the feminine form "Phocis"
used in the original. This is the right Greek form for the country,
whereas "Phocas" would be the proper form in which to designate
a man of Phocis. A correspondent had raised this point in a letter
to F.B.B., but J.A. was totally unaware of it.

THE STORY OF EAWULF

Note.—During excavation alongside the south aisle footing of the nave, in continuation of the work on the south-west tower footings, an interment of a curious nature was encountered. The skeleton lay in the clay just outside the wall, and the head was protected by a "dropstone" having a cylindrical hollow, open at the neck, in which lay the skull. Between the legs of the skeleton was a second skull, but broken. At the foot was a flat stone laid across, and against it on the further side a number of leg-bones, etc. The following was written shortly after the discovery:

SITTING XXXIV. 19th September, 1908.

"Radulphus Cancellarius, who slew Eawulf in fair fight, did nevertheless suffer by his foeman's seaxe, which broke his bones asunder.[1] He, dying after many years, desired that they who loved him should bury him without the church where he was wont to feed the birds in his chair. The sunne did shine there, as he loved it, for his blood was cold." "It is strange, yet wee know it is true. The head of Eawulf was (there). As they digged around his body they knew not that the head of Eawulf fell, and so lay betwixt his feet. And thus have ye found it.

"I, Gulielmus, I knew the old church that Radulphus did pull downe, and much lieth beneath the floor of ye newe church. Search estward of where ye now digge and ye shall find much, and of the old work made they the vaults, and some are deeper. Be not deceived by appear-

---

[1] The right forearm was afterwards found to be fractured.

ances. Under where ye now think is the end of all, there will be seen very deep walls of the older church. None knew of them, and they were not destroyed. Seek also north of the said cutting: there is somewhat there ye might not know of."

Q. " Why was the head of Radulphus protected by a dropstone, when the body was not enclosed ?"

A. " Soe he wished it. Let the worms of the earth devour my poor body with all its sinnes, saith he. Mine head did ever fight against the body. It is the best part of me. See ye, saith he, that ye protect it! That foul body—let hym go, saith hee."

Q. " How did Eawulf come to be buried there, and who was he ?"

A. " Know ye not Eawulf, the Yarl of Edgarley, of royal blood, who harried the Norman, and would have slain Turstinus ?[1] A doughty Saxon he, and one who said that Glaston was builded by the Saxon, and Saxon it should remain. So he was buried in Glaston, and not in his own chapel at Edgarley.[2] The holy men of Glaston, they who were of Saxon blood, suffered much through his violence in their behalf, and, God wot, through no rebellion of their own ; and they had their reward, for a Saxon[3] again was Abbot for a time."

[1] Radulphus Cancellarius. This we supposed, at first, to refer to the great Radulphus or Ralph (FitzStephen), who was responsible for the rebuilding of the Abbey Church after the great fire of 1184; but this would be eighty-three years after the time of Turstin, first Norman Abbot (1082-1101). Malmesbury tells us of the trouble that ensued from the tyrannical methods of Turstin, and the slaughter of the monks by hired soldiers. But the story of Eawulf is new.

[2] Eawulf, Yarl of Edgarley. The name was quite unknown to us. Edgarley is about a mile out of Glastonbury on the southeast. There is an ancient chapelry there, dedicated to St. Dunstan. Subsequent reference to the Anglo-Saxon Chronicles brought to light the following entry under date A.D. 885:

" Eanwulf, Earl of *Somerton,* buried in Glastonbury Abbey." Somerton is about six miles from Glastonbury on the same side as Edgarley—*i.e.,* south. This is interesting, as suggesting a family name perpetuated for some six generations, or about 200 years, in the district.

[3] Turstin, whose violence caused his dismissal by the King, and exile for a time to Normandy, was succeeded by Herlewin, whose Saxon name receives interesting corroboration by the script.

SITTING XXXVII.   23rd September, 1908.

Q. " How is the great difference in date between Radulphus and Eawulf to be explained ?   We cannot reconcile this."

A. " Wee know not your dates, nor the tymes gone by ; but this we know—Eawulf and Radulphus[1] did fight, and the Norman did slay the Saxon.   This is fact, as we know it   Be sure of your own tymes and look at Domesday for light.

" We remember (Radulphus) was an hundred years and three when he went to hys fathers :—hale and of a good visage even then—but hys bones did grieve him (by reason of) ye payne in them.   Soe did he seek ye sunne.   More we will serche in the great army of past things.   They are soe hard to find !

" That wych is hidden will be found out and all ye Abbaye is at your hands ; but serche.   Alle three churches are open to ye, and one whych was of old time in the midst of the nave of ye newe—not much, for Turstinus did remove . . . them when he builded anewe the Norman churche " (*i.e.*, built the new Norman church.—F.B.B.).

Q. " Did Eawulf lead the assault in the fight ?   How did it come about ?"

A. " Old men have strong anger, but youth should have spared him.   More we know not,—we wil serche."

The script here breaks off into the description (already given) of the pilgrims' procession at sunset, with the music of organs and bells.

SITTING XLII.   18th April, 1911.

The problem of the dates was left for further consideration, and remained in abeyance for two and a half years.   At this sitting other matters of early history had been touched upon, and it

[1] Written " Turstinus."

occurred to F.B.B. to ask a question as to Radulphus and Eawulf.

Q. "Please explain the apparent discrepancy of dates in the story of Radulphus and his fight with Eawulf."

A. "**Ne Radulphus of Henry the King**" (*i.e.*, Fitz-Stephen, 1184.—F.B.B.). "**Radulphus the Treasurer was Norman of the time of Turstinus—annos One Thousand and Eighty-seven. Ralph was hee. Eorwulf of Edgarley, old in years, was wroth because the soldiers of Turstinus did slay the Saxon monks. Ralph the Norman knight and Treasurer of Turstinus, slew him. Who was hee? Radulphus FitzHamon—as wee wot, an evil man.**"

Q. "Where was Ralph FitzStephen—of Henry II.—buried?"

A. "**Ralph, ye cousin of ye King, dyed as we deem, at Wincastre—there yburied. Chancellor of Angleland was he.**"

Note.—The two foregoing answers were now read, but unfortunately the first was incorrectly interpreted, as the writing was a little difficult. F.B.B. made the mistake of thinking that it implied that Ralph of Turstinus was FitzStephen (though the sense is clear enough on further inspection), and consequently asked as follows:

Q. "Why do you say that Ralph, treasurer of Turstinus, was Ralph of King Henry?"

(Here the influence changes and a masterful "personality" of whom we have had previous experience, controls the utterance.)

A. "**Rede. I said it not. I said not 'Ralph of the King Henricus,' but 'Ralph ye Norman.' Taedet damnosum. Lege!—IMPERATOR.**

"**Audi me, barbari stultissimi! Ego Imperator, qui feci interpretationes pro anima insularium.—CAESAR.**"[1]

---

[1] Which may be freely translated as : "Listen to me, you very dull barbarians !—to me, the Emperor, who have been trying to make these things clear to the minds of you islanders."

PART III

THE LORETTO CHAPEL

PLATE IV.

CONEY'S VIEW OF THE ABBEY (1817).

THE LORETTO CHAPEL

AMONG the lost features of Glastonbury Abbey recorded by Leland[1] is a chapel built by Abbot Bere on the north side of the nave. Leland says of this:

"Bere cumming from his Embassadrie out of Italie[2] made a Chapelle of our Lady de Loretta, joining to the north side of the body of the Church."

But apart from his record, which has preserved the bare memory of the work and its approximate location, we have no surviving facts, either historical or descriptive, to guide us in the search for its vestiges, save one or two trifles which the orthodox archæologist would probably despise, but on which the imagination might build an airy and tenuous fabric, a mere gossamer which the rude touch of practical argument would dispel, and which would find its place more fittingly in the pages of romance than in the chronicles of the labours of serious-minded antiquaries.

Here, then, was a chance for the supraliminal mind to exercise its powers, just the opportunity most desirable for an experiment in the psychology of inductive and deductive processes, and a test

---

[1] *Itinerary*, vol. iii., p. 103.
[2] Undertaken in 1503, on the election of Pius III.

of the possibility of drawing by the thread of slenderest and most imperfect knowledge, some kindred knowledge from the great reservoir of the memory of nature. This experiment was made, and the result of it I am going to give my readers without any sort of reticence or reserve, making no claim, but asking that they will regard it with an open mind, and accepting it for analysis as an illustration of the working of the latent powers of the mind under the same conditions that we in the onset laid down for our work.

The material from which our sublimated essence was distilled was as follows:

1. Leland's note, as above.

2. A fragment of walling shown in Coney's view of the Abbey, 1817. This appears in the sketch just on the spot where the wall of the north aisle of the nave would have joined that of the transept at its eastern extremity, but it is diminutive in height—only about a third of the height proper to the nave wall, as is clearly evident by comparison with the surrounding features. It is like a little screen-wall, and such as might have filled at one time an archway at this point opening from the last or most eastward division of the north aisle wall towards a chapel just without, in the angle between the aisle and the north transept. But in Coney's sketch it does not look like a Gothic work, but is more like a building of the modern times, since it has four little dumpy windows with round heads and the projecting cills which we associate with our everyday ex-

perience of domestic building. No one but Coney, so far as I am aware, has indicated any sort of remnant of building at this point, and there are several older views of the Abbey, which would be expected to show it if anything had been there. Look, for example, at Stukeley's panoramic view of the ruins, published in 1723. (See Fig. 10, p. 115.) Nothing visible there—the whole of the north side of the nave an open field, as it had been for at least half a century previous (*vide* Hollar's view).

3. In the Cannon MS., a diary referring to Glastonbury about the time of George II., is a sketch plan of the Abbey, very crude, in which the writer shows a mound of rubbish and rough stones with suggestions of a broken wall on the ground at or near this point, and he makes a note to the effect that it is the remains of " The Chapter House."

But, of course, the Chapter House was on the south side of the Choir, and could not have been elsewhere in the case of Glastonbury, as its site was never in doubt, and it has now been recovered and its dimensions tested and proved.

4. Marsh, the old gardener at the Abbey for over forty years, used to say to me that in the grass bank which runs along the north side of the nave area, under the trees, there was a fine bit of freestone walling, some of which Mr. Austin, his earlier employer, used up for building. I dug in, but could find nothing of this at the point he indicated.

Now, at the risk of being a little tedious, I pro-

8

pose to quote a short paragraph from my *Archi-*
tectural Handbook, because it shows what I was
thinking about this matter in 1910, and such evidence is needed for any useful analysis of the
psychology of the whole subsequent matter.

I would add that, so far as I can remember, my
friend J.A. had formed no theory as to the nature
of the chapel or its real position other than my
own, and what I here quote represents the utmost
that could at the time be said (*Architectural Hand-*
book of Glastonbury Abbey, second edition, pp. 32,
33, 1910):

"Some fragments of building on the north side
of the nave were surviving as recently as 1817,
when Coney's drawings were published. In one
of these we see a wall with a row of windows having
a rather unusual detail in their heads (Fig. 10).
This would be near the site of the Loretto Chapel,
built by Abbot Bere. Carter, writing some few
years later, tells us that the Loretto Chapel was
then standing, and if he be correct, it must have
been a substantial piece of masonry exterior to the
church, and not a light internal structure within it,
as has been conjectured. But he may have been
referring to the Chapel of Saint Thomas the Martyr
in the north transept, which has sometimes been
miscalled the 'Loretto Chapel.'

"A sketch plan in the Cannon MS. shows a group
of ruins in an apparently similar position, and he
records the tradition of a very magnificent building at this point, which he terms the 'Chapter
House.' However erroneous this designation, we

FIG. 10.—VIEW OF THE RUINS IN 1723. (From Stukeley's Itinerary.)

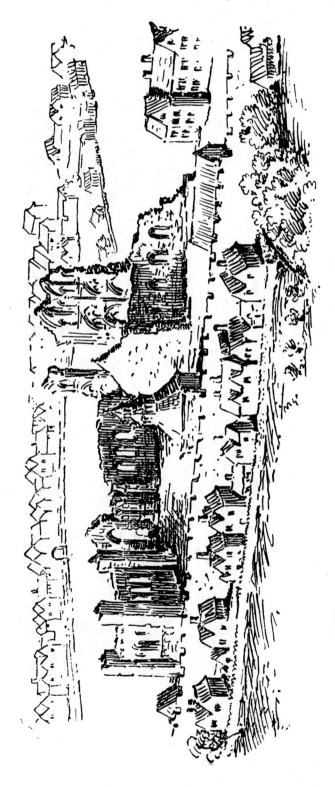

Fig. 11.—Glastonbury Abbey in 1655 *circa*: Enlargement of Hollar's View.

Fig. 12.—MS. Plan of John Cannon, 1740 *circa*.

A, Chaple; *B*, quire; *C*, the great arch; *D*, the nave or body; *E*, the chapter house; *F*, gate to ye kitchen; *G*, St. Joseph's Chaple.

may at least accept his record as corroborative of the existence of a richly ornamented building of some special nature (as distinct from the body of the Church at the junction of the Nave aisle and North Transept)."

It seems, then, that we had formed the impression of a fine building just outside the nave wall and in the angle of aisle and transept; but to be strictly accurate, I do not think that Coney's sketch had much weight as regards the character of the work it might have contained, and so far as one's normal impressions were concerned, it was dismissed as " modern."

RECORD OF·EXCAVATION IN 1911.

In the early part of June, 1911, the footing trench of the north aisle wall of the nave was opened up at its eastward end, and the junction of the same with the west wall of the north transept was found. The area just outside the angle of the two walls was cleared with the object of discovering traces of a chapel at this point, but beyond a few very beautiful sections of window mullions of the style of the late fifteenth or early sixteenth century—good Tudor work—nothing material came to light in the way of detail. But about 13 feet west of the transept wall, and running parallel to it, meeting the line of the aisle wall at right angles and going north from it, was found another broad foundation, and this we assumed at the time to be the footing of the west wall of the Loretto Chapel.   The inference was clear that there must at least have been some building of a permanent nature, and rather substantial, attached to the west face of the transept wall just outside its junction with the aisle, and perhaps it was not unreasonable at the time to suppose that this was the Loretto Chapel.   The architectural detail discovered pointed to a Gothic chapel, and was entirely inconsistent with such a building as Coney showed.   Neither was it of like character with the work in the Nave.   Such was the position when, on 13th June, 1911, we obtained the following automatic script:

SITTING XLVII.   13th June, 1911.

" I made that building.   All that I didde anywhere is fannes.   Ne barrel vault.   And under them, three faire windowes of foure lights with transomes and littel castel-work on the ramps thereof.   And if ye digge in the wall of the navis, there is much fell in.   Serche the great pier of the nave opposite the cutte: yt is full . . . but they threw therein the fragments of my capella, a canopy at the west, and all the central ones—faire canopy work, and in the midst a littel one for Our Ladye, sylver guilt and very faire.   Somewhat remaineth of ye outer walls and ye walle by ye crossinge, but they have taken hym mostly away long syne.   Very deepe fannes . . . and each fanne had twelve ribs, and they were ycoloured red and gold, like my chapel of Edgar.   There yet remaineth somewhat of Our Ladye.   Yt lieth in front of the west walle three feet or thereabouts.   Seek ye well out the bank to the Est: something remaineth of ye transept (?) wall whereon we placed the tabernacles, but most is ygone.   Ye doore unto hym is at the west,[1] nigh unto the pillar of the navis, one doore only, on nave.

[1] This must be a mistake.   The south is the Nave side.—F.B.B.

" R. B. scripsit, pro instructionem tuam.   Ye roundels
of ye volte were golden, and also ye bosses, and ye hollows
were bright redde ; likewise ye tabernacle of Oure Ladye
in the est wall golde and redde ; and ye windowes were of
glasse yellow in canopies with redde and blewe in ye little
lights thereof.   Ye floore was of tileis red, with shields, and
ornaments in yellow likewise, and it was very faire and
magnifical, like unto my chappel of Edgar, but more faire,
for I builded hym later, for I hadde a vowe of mine owne
which I performed."

Q. " What was your vow ?"

A. " Know ye not that wee were borne downe by rude
men in foreign parts and the mule which bore me fell,
for I was a grete and heavy man.   And being like to fall
down a steepe place or be trampled by ye mule, I called
on Oure Lady and shee heard me, soe that my cloke catch-
ing on a thorne I was prevented, and then said I : ' Lo!
When I returne I will build a chapel to Our Lady of the
Loretto, and soe instant was I inn (my vowe) that the
brethren were grieved, for yt was arranged in Chapitre
that wee shold build a Chapel to oure Edgare before I
wennt in ye shyppe.   Therefore builded I hym first, for
it was a public vowe : but mine owne vowe I fulfilled
afterer, and soe all was well—Yt is given."

Q. " What was the occasion of your journey ?"

A. " Know ye not of my Ambassadrie, when ye Kinge
wold know what the Bis^p of Roume would doe ?   Even soe
journeying fromm Padua whither came the shippes, we
felle among evil menne who would hold us to ransome.
Here fell ye mule, and ye reste ye knowe."

NOTES ON BEERE'S EMBASSY.

Abbot Richard Bere was deputed by Henry
VII. to visit Rome in 1503, in order, it is said,
to congratulate the new Pope, Pius III., on his
election.   Whether there was any political object
intended to be served by his embassy does not

appear, but it is strongly suggested by subsequent events. The new Pope did not live to establish his policy. He survived his election only twenty-six days, and was succeeded during the same year by Julius II., a "political" Pope, who formed the "League of Cambrai," which was followed by the "Holy League" of powers against Louis XII. of France, including England, Spain, and Venice in the bond, which Henry VIII. afterwards joined, until the peace with France in 1514 ended it. As to the story of the journey, the mention of Padua as his port of call seemed odd, and a little hard to understand. The usual route to Rome for English travellers of that period was via Antwerp, Augsbourg, and Venice. From Venice he might have taken boat to the wharves of Padua, and would thence proceed southward along the Adriatic side, till near Ancona, and here he would strike Loreto, which would be the start of an overland journey, the Apennines being crossed possibly on mule-back.

Q. "What were the dimensions of the work about which you have been telling us?"

A. "Yn feete twenty and two, and foure paces in width thereof, and ye walle of ye nave was strengthened thereby, for ye towre hadde pressed ye walls through the volt of the navis, and hee was crackt all ye way to the bottom thereof. Therefore my chapel was high, in height twenty and three feet, and very strong in the volt, soe that it tied the wall of ye nave and ye wall of ye crossing where it was weake. They who builded ye towre should have made arches in ye walle to help ye higher windowes, carrying them along ye crossing in ye walle to helpe ye towre at ye angle, but they did not. Therefore helped I yt by my chappell and by an arche I builded from ye toppe of ye aisle to the roofe of ye chappell to bond ye whole at ye angle. Also builded I ye grete arches in ye towre. It wasne ye volte that did caste out, but ye towre gave inne as against ye volte by reason of its weight,[1] and soe it even gave away from[2] the crossing in its lowre part and gave out in its upper.—R. B."

Q. " Can you give us an idea of the state of opinion in the religious establishments of your day—of the views and ideals current ?"

A. " Ne helde I wyth superstitions. Ever I was for ye people and ye better understanding of ye mysteries. It was meet that it be soe, and notte kept in the hearts of the religious only. More wold ye ? What more I didde as seemed best, for the old tymes were changing and menne loved the glory of our ceremonial. They were angered at the deceits which hadde kept their fathers humble and meek. Through the eye the glory of our services might make them wish for noble things, but I knew, and hee my friend knew[3] they were no longer to be fooled with trickery. All was changing in my day and the wars made for greater knowledge. The Englyshe were (a)sleepe no more, ne ever to be. Dixi."

The dimensions given for this little chapel could be applied to the foundations discovered only if the longer measure (22 feet) were taken north and south, and the shorter (four paces) east and west. This would make the building cover one bay of the transept, and extend to the outer footing wall exposed by the excavation. But this footing did not stop at 22 feet, but ran on north, and was found to be co-extensive with the northerly projection of the transept, so that the chapel described would only have occupied one-half of the length,

---

[1] This seems perfectly true. The great piers buckled under the weight of the tower, and bowed inwards, probably pushing the vault, and cracking it by compression.—F.B.B.

[2] *Gave in towards* the crossing would be more expressive of the fact.—F.B.B.   [3] Bere was the friend of Erasmus.

and it looked as if there had been an aisle to the transept such as F.B.B. showed in his drawing of the reconstructed interior. The description of the strongly built little chapel in the angle, buttressing up the weak tower and transept wall, was a plausible one, but the description, and especially the dimensions, would not throw any light on Coney's sketch, and left the wall in the bank, spoken of by the gardener, still unexplained. The dimensions were small—unsatisfying for a special work of this nature, and one which had merited individual mention by Leland. And the proportion was so unusual, in that the east and west measurement was the lesser and would be insufficient for its purpose, one would think, unless the altar were placed at the north end, which would not be an English custom. Was this little building, after all, the real Chapel of the Loretto, or was it only an antechamber, through which access would be had from the nave to a more important work farther out? The long aisle-like footing looked like an adit or approach. It could hardly have been part of the transept because of the sharp difference in level between the two floors, that of the transept being 4 feet or so above the nave. But only further digging could bring light, and this was at the time impossible, so there the matter was bound to remain until a more favourable opportunity should occur for further research. So it rested for five years.

In December, 1916, F.B.B. and J.A. found themselves near neighbours, and it had been mutually agreed, in view of the greatly revived interest in the subject of spiritual phenomena, that the experiments in writing should be resumed, but no definite day had been fixed. Some days before F.B.B. had given J.A. some MS. notes to transcribe, being extracts he had made some years before from the Cannon MS. It had been proposed to publish these in the *Proceedings of the Somerset Archæological Society*, and with them was the sketch of the ruins already referred to, at which both had casually glanced; but this had not been the subject of attention. and J.A.'s transcript had not arrived at that point when the first sitting was held. This was on 4th December. Glastonbury matters were not to the fore in recent conversation, which had been given to the subject of the Greek Cabala and the geometry connected with it. J.A. says his mind was still full of this on 4th December, to the exclusion of Glastonbury, and that the reference in the Cannon MS. had not been in his thoughts. F.B.B.'s experience was similar. He had been busy with letters until the moment of J.A.'s arrival, and his last envelope having been sealed, he, on the spur of the moment, proposed a sitting, to which J.A. agreed. F.B.B. had an idea that if any writing were obtained it might be on the subject of the war and current events; and J.A. anticipated something on geometrical symbolism. No suggestion was made as to the subject of the proposed communication. The following is the record:

SITTING. 4th December, 1916.

The first page of writing is cramped and well-nigh illegible. The following can be made out:

" Cosmic facts are everywhere, but not easily attained. . . .

" . . . by assembling yourselves together and obtaining the inspiration ye seek consciously or unconsciously. The result obtained is the same, but the word endures. . . .

" . . . The material world is the screen between—the complex fabric of the simple weaving. The essential facts are eternal which (? move) in a circle, and to them that know the circle, somewhat will pass into all times, only ye see but little at a time. The centre is the point on which all revolves, and ye, revolving, are conscious of the influence, but cannot know the radius. . . ."

" Obliviscor. So long we have slept near Capella Loretta under the bank full thirty paces from the Navis. Ye did not go farre enow beyond the (bank) they cast up there. It was full five feet in, and buried in the place where he didd drawe the Chapitre Howse.[1] and the end of the pilgrimmes (way) is . . . through ye porche, thro ye wicket gate in ye corner, and by ye steppes over against ye lower graveyard. There shewed wee the relics and ye pilgrimmes passed by this way to the Chapell of St. Mary, by ye steppes, and to Navis majoure."

Then in a different hand:

" Abbot Bere ybuilded ye Loretto Chapel faire and large to the north (side of the) navis. We said that itt . . . was not ye Chapitre Howse. . . .

" . . . The syde of it was distant from ye navis thirty-one feet and a half, and from ye aisle of ye transept he was fulle tenn feet with a covered way unto, and four steppes up unto ye aisle aforesaid. Yt . . . was ybuilded by Bere most faire and wonderfull in ye newe style brought from Ytaly when he didd goe there upon ambassadrie.

" Ye have heard of yt. Ye Chapell was full forty feet,

[1] This appears to be in allusion to the note in the Cannon MS. which J.A. says he had not then noticed.

and width between twenty and . . . twenty-one feet, and
hee had an entrance unto (hym) from the roade which
ledde from St. John his gait unto ye navis, and thus
might ye Bᵖ and the Kinges majestie (enter).

" Bere used to approach by entering into the Claustre,
and soe he didde close it oftentimes."

The foregoing script at first sight seemed impossible to decipher, and a repetition was asked
for. This was clearly written, and by its aid the
sense of the foregoing was mastered, and word by
word picked out, but there are yet some seemingly
hopeless blanks. These, however, may not be
material, and will probably refer to the ruinous
state of the Chapter House and its repair, as
re-stated in the following communication:

" We have said he was of the Ytalian style new and very
faire, and Bere ybuilded coming from embassadrie in
Ytaly. Hee was not ye Chapitre, but Bere did use hym
so because ye Chaptre House was dammp and ruinous
and was being repaired. We have said so. Hee met ye
King and ye Bᵖ who sojourned (with him). The same
was forty feet (long) by twenty (or) thereabouts and his
grylled doore was to the west and a pavement joyned him
to the Road from St. John's gate to ye churche.

" He wasne like anything else (but was of the) newe
style. There were four steppes—nay, six—to the aisle
of ye transeppt, and a covered way vaulted in a rounde
vaulte to ye Chappell. . . .—THESIGER."

Q. " By ' steps ' do you mean ascending steps, or paces ?"

A. " Ten feet, and four or six steppes up to hym."

The signature " THESIGER " is of peculiar
interest. At the beginning of this communication will be seen the words " Obliviscor."
" So long we have slept near Capella Loretta,"
etc. Only once before, at Sitting XLII., on the

7th September, 1910, has the same signature been observed. This was at the close of a communication dealing with the shrine of St. Dunstan, and was given as follows:

" Sub marmore dormio, quod taedet me—obliviscor.—
CAMILLUS THESIGER."

The identity of this person was at the time a matter of speculation, but F.B.B. concluded that it must be meant for Camel, the Purse-bearer to Abbot Bere, whose marble tomb with coffered panels is a feature in St. John's Church. Camel had a house in the upper part of the town, in the High Street, on the south side, some little way above St. John's Gate, and to the east.

The architectural details which we here reproduce were then given, some explanatory notes appended.

THE LORETTO CHAPEL

ARCHITECTURAL PLANS

DESCRIPTION OF PLAN A.

I. *a*, Drawing of a gable with " stepped " coping, probably meant for the west gable.

I. *b*, Plan of the Chapel, showing four bays in length, with buttresses having a pointed profile, labelled " Cappella Loretta."

I. *c*, Elevation of a circular-headed recess, with ornament in head, labelled " Cava."

I. *d*, Plan (enlarged) of the Chapel, showing an entrance ("portus") apparently in the south-west bay.

DESCRIPTION OF PLAN B.

I. *e*, Plan of the east end of Chapel, showing the convex " Cava Virginis," and the door ("portus") leading to the church.

I. *f*, Another and clearer plan of the Chapel, confirming the four-bay division.

I. *g*, Elevation of the east wall of Chapel, as seen internally, the " Cava Virginis," or semicircular recess, being in the centre and the door to the transept on the right or south side.

PLAN A.

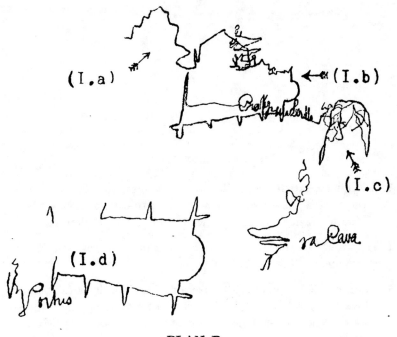

(I.a)

(I.b)

(I.c)

(I.d)

Portus

ra Cava

PLAN B.

I.(f.)

I (e.)

Portus

portus ad ecclesiam

I.(g)

DESCRIPTION OF PLAN C.

I. *h*, This appears to be another effort to show the east wall, but the " Cava " is so small that the alternative suggests itself of an elevation of the west wall, with a central doorway.

I. *j*, *k*, Head of the " Cava," with attempt to represent a shell ornament filling the hollow of same.

II. *a*, Elevation, probably of exterior of west wall, with round-headed door, and " Virgo " over—*i.e.*, a statue of the Virgin here. There is a suggestion of undulating parapets, with a sitting lion at the corner.

II. *b*, *c*, Divisions of the copings, with lions at intervals.

PLAN C.

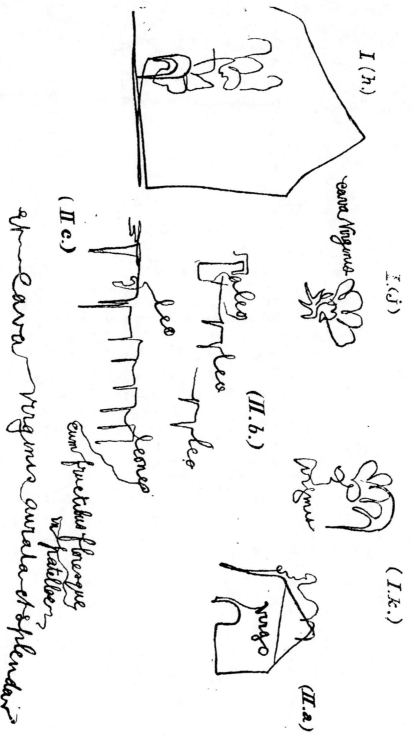

I (h.)

cava Virginis

I (j)

(I.k.)

(II.b.)

leo

Virginis

virgo

(II.a)

(II c.)

leo
leo
leo

cum fructibus floreaque
in platibus

cava virginis aurata et splendens

DESCRIPTION OF PLAN D.

II. *d*, Another drawing of the east end of the plan, with the position of the east door, written " portus ad ecclesiam et voltus quadripartus." Note " portus " for " porta," and " voltus " for " volta," always occurring in these writings.

II. *e*, *f*, Repetition of the undulating contours of the parapet, labelled " parapetus." The lions at intervals as before.

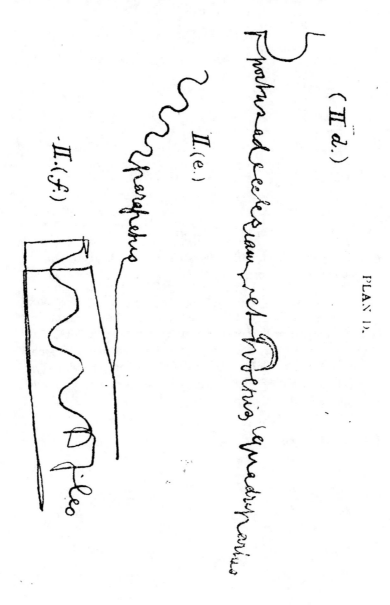

PLAN D.

DESCRIPTION OF PLAN E.

II. *g*, Undulating outline of a parapet, with foliage ornament applied, and the word " leo."

II. *h*, Sketch of a small pier or baluster form. This is labelled " patella and pillar." The word " patella " has the same intention as the word " patera," well known as an architectural term and implying a plate or panel, often of rectangular form. This may be let into the surface of a pilaster. The plan clearly indicates a flat pier or pilaster; or it may imply an abacus for the support of the lion.

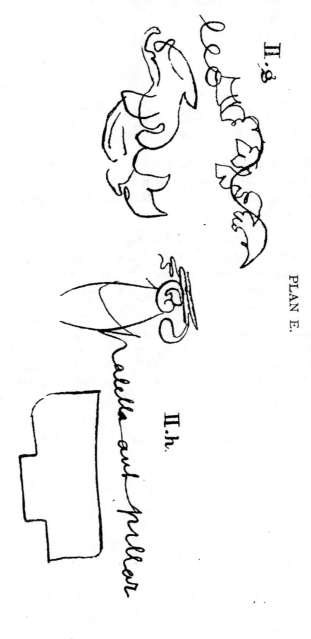

PLAN E.

II. g.

II. h.

DESCRIPTION OF PLAN F.

III. *a*, Two sketches of the lions. They are sitting lions, holding shields, as we see them in many Tudor buildings, but the ornament is more customary in domestic work than in ecclesiastical.

III. *b*, More parapets, this time partly of a Florentine pattern. Whether these are meant for a more detailed study of the undulations previously shown, or are some in a special position, does not yet appear. The little " angels " seem to be connected with them.

III. *c*, Probably meant for one of the heads of the side-windows in the Chapel. There is clearly a semicircle at head, and there appears some sort of filling like open scroll-work. No English precedent of this date is known to the writer.

PLAN F.

(III.a)

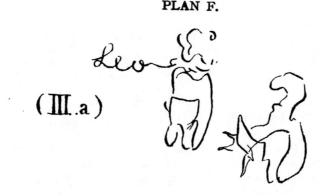

(b.)

(c)

Description of Plan G.

III. *d*, Another sketch of the " Cava," with the description of the treatment of its recess: " Golden stars on azure, at the back of the Virgin's Hollow "; and it proceeds: " Ad orientem, in cava Virginis Mari(a)e Lorettae quod . . . ad ecclesiam . . . via claustra ad eccl^m . . . ad orientem . . . ad ecclesiam " (To the east, a covered way, or cloister, leading to the church).

III. *e*, Again a plan of the east end of the Chapel, with the door marked " portus," and a line going east.

III. *f*, The " via claustra " shown from the Chapel to the " ecclesia."

PLAN G.

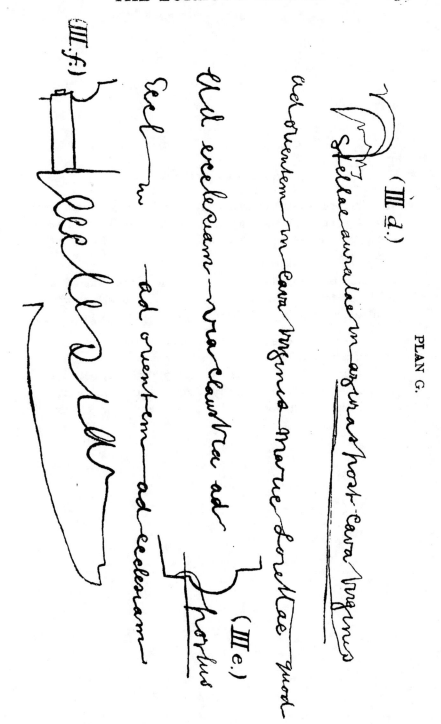

DESCRIPTION OF PLAN H.

IV. *a,* "Chapel is forty (in) feet by twenty." Then follows an elevation of one side showing the round heads of the windows connected by a string-course, and the writing " forty feet, four parts."

IV. *b,* Sketch of a rounded vault, its groin carved along the whole length. Described thus : " Volt of fruit and flowers painted very cunningly. Ye ribs of volts ycarven so."

IV. *c,* Small sketch of one of the sitting lions at the angle of the Chapel, with one crenelle of the parapet adjoining. Described thus: " Ye Lèones cornerwise, and thre(e) between. The partitions were 10 feet, forty in length and twenty wide," with round vaults: ribs carven with fruit and many colours.

PLAN H.

(IV. a.) chapel ~ forty feet by twenty ft.

forty feet four parts

(IV. b.) roof of fruit and flowers painted very cunningly perfectly carved

40 dores concave and three between

(IV. c.) the ... 10 feet forty in length and twenty wide

PLAN I.

(IV. d.)

with windvaultts ribs
Leones   carven with fruitt
and many colours

IV. *d*, Another sketch of a sitting lion.

REVIEW.

It was with a sense of astonishment that, after so great a lapse of time, this interesting communication, so voluminous in detail, and so apparently explanatory of doubts and difficulties in connection with the obscure problem of the Loretto Chapel, should have presented itself unsought, unexpected, and inclusive of strange new elements which suggested the existence at Glastonbury in Bere's day of an architectural model which would be unique for the period in these islands, and probably without parallel in Northern Europe.

Several questions arise in the mind. Could the little windows in Coney's sketch have stimulated a subconscious dream of an Italian chapel? But where are we to look for the original model of these undulating parapets, Lions sejeant with shields, patellæ, fruit and flower enrichment, the conchoidal "Cava Virginis," and the precision of the general proportions? Was there, in the subconscious memory of either of the sitters, some forgotten impression of a building in Padua or elsewhere in Northern Italy, which in its main features, or subsidiary detail, might tally with what was here given? That we cannot say, for nothing of the sort could or can be recalled by the conscious mind.

Should the day come when the bank of rubble on the north side of the nave of Glastonbury Abbey can be thoroughly explored, it may be that beyond some traces of the freestone wall spoken of by the old gardener there may be found *nothing*; but if, on the other hand, it should appear that by the same obscure mental process which has already, in the case of the Edgar Chapel, predicated the existence, with practical truth in form and detail, of a building whose very memory was lost (and the evidence for which had been ignored, nay even scouted, by the most competent antiquaries), another architectural treasure, long buried and forgotten, might once again be brought to light, and its wealth of Italian detail verified; then, indeed, would come into sight new vistas, new possibilities of exploration and research into the secrets of old time, and we should stand at the threshold of the Gate of Remembrance.

SITTING.   16th August, 1917 (at Gloucester).

Note.—The objects sought in this communication were formulated by F.B.B. in advance. They chiefly concerned the discrepancies between the two descriptions of Bere's buildings given at previous sittings, 13th June, 1911, and 4th December, 1916, the first of which referred to some work unidentified. F.B.B. suggested that the discovery of the footings of the transept "aisle" immediately before the former of these two sittings had created a mental bias in favour of a "chapel" there, and thus confused the script.

" Maestro . . . Francesco de Padua qui me instruxit et capella(m) cognoscit in Italia. Ille etiam scripsit cum me et ille . . . (struebat) in modo Italiano, et mecum in nave navigavit ad Brit(tanniam). Ille aedificavit et ornavit."

" Deepe, by ye Bank, is ye walle where ye fathers didde sit in their old age ; and they had not the use[1] of the younger brethren, but were free—and who wished to spend hys dayes in ease and luxury ? But capella wasne in muro in Boreali parte. I have told ye. It was soe, and in the banke deepe down ye shall find hym full perfect as I do think. There was a deepe place where they destroyed and they covered him and made a banke full six feet high, and soe saved the wall at the west end for all tyme.

" Ask ye, what was the chapel under the Tower beyond the Porche ? He was for the reliquaries, and ye did enter hym from the garth on the syde of St. Mary's and uppe four steppes to him, and soe through to the upper garth and ye road to the John's Gate."

*   *   *   *   *

[1] *I.e.*, did not keep the canonical hours, etc.—F.B.B.

" Wysdom—it was best soe. The Land was ycovered with the houses of God, and the grass he could not grow, and it was in the providence of God that the houses were destroyed, for they held no life. Men desired fuller life in ye world, and to travel far ; and the old faith[1] was no longer needed, for the minds of men were no longer as ye beasts that perish, but each man was a light unto himself and did need no father to control him—so it was best, though much loveliness was destroyed in the undoing. The Spirit liveth still, and what we lived for, in new guise we give to you. Grow in the Spirit. We are a symbol of great truths, and ye read the symbol aright. That which we did dream lives on, and in the Spirit we pass it on to you, from symbol to symbol—ever higher, ever wider.

" As great books were we, and our work was in stone— a language handed down for you to read, which we had forgotten, and so fell.

" What wold ye?"

At this point there was a pause in the writing. Neither F.B.B. nor J.A. were aware of anything that had been written. The sheets were replaced and laid aside as they were filled, and nothing was suggested during the writing by either sitter. There was a little conversation on other subjects. At this point it occurred to F.B.B. (though in ignorance of the question " What wold ye ?") to ask the following, and he wrote it down on the paper.

Q. " Do you confirm all that was told us of the Italian design of the chapel of the Loretto ? Please say what building in Italy was the model chosen by Abbot Richard Bere for this work."

A. " Francesco de Padua aedificavit. Two would speak of it—he who made it and I who moved for my fannes: ' English. We both made hym—I, and he, my friend."

---

[1] *I.e.*, the old system.

"Capella di Marco[1] at Padua—hym by the Key.[2]
"Dominic di Vallera Castiglione[3] aedificavit anno 1497
—via St. Ursula."

At this point the sitting was broken off and
resumed on the evening following—17th August,
1917.

*Q. by F.B.B. "Please tell us plainly, what was the build-
ing 22 feet long and 4 paces wide spoken of on 13th June,
1911 ? What was its use and what was its dedication ?
This is the building with the fan-vaulting. Tell us exactly
where it stood."*

"Vincula ecclesiae disrupta sunt. Claustra aperta
sunt.

"Claustra quae vocantur, vento Boreali aperta est (*sic*)[4]
in vestibulo sub turre—English volts—and Capella Lorettae
(in) Ytaliano modo.

"Capella Loretta was on ye lower level, with four or six
steppys up to the pavement. One steppe to hym from the
way from John's Gate to the North Porche.

"Seek my chapple as I told ye in ye Banck. He was
entered from ye West, and had a door into the littel
cloister by ye transept of ye grete Church, and four stepps
up to the pavement.

"Ye door was in ye transept wall at ye end thereof.

"Wold ye have many things ? The Vineyard was by
the Ponds behind the Priests' Houses that I ybuilded, over
against the (road ?), and beyond ye gallery at the Maudlin

[1] Not mentioned in Cesare Foligno's *Story of Padua*, but
there is a chapel of St. Mark figured in a mediæval map of the
town. The mention of this saint tends to explain the lions
mentioned in the 1916 script, which had hitherto seemed an
incongruous feature, if not quite out of place on a chapel of Our
Lady.—F.B.B.

[2] The Chapel of St. Mark occupies, in the map, a place not far
from the river, and near the mediæval bridge of St. Mathio. As
the River Bacchiglione was navigable, it seems quite probable
that there would be quays along its banks within the city.

[3] This name is quite unknown to either of us.—F.B.B.

[4] Evidently a play upon words, the first "Claustra" apparently signifying that the barred gates are opened; and the
second, "that which we should describe as 'cloisters' were open
at this point to the North Wind."

Gate by the water. On ye side of ye grete Courte was ye brick yarde—beyond ye fishponds. Seek ye foundations at ye east of ye great Court where ye pryor's chapel was, and I ybuilded in front of hym. Digge also near by the Kitchens, which were near together.

"That which the brethren of old handed down to us, we followed, ever building on their plann. As we have said, our Abbey was a message in ye stones. In ye foundations and ye distances be a mystery—the mystery of our Faith, which ye have forgotten and we also in ye latter days.

"All ye measures were marked plaine on ye slabbes in Mary's Chappel,[1] and ye have destroyed them. So it was recorded, as they who builded and they who came after knew aforehand where they should build. But these things are overpast and of no value now. The spirit was lost and with the loss of the spirit the body decayed and was of no further use to (us).

"There was the Body of Christ, and round him would have been the Four Ways. Two were ybuilded and no more. In ye floor of ye Mary Chappel was ye Zodiac, that all might see and understand the mystery. In ye midst of ye Chapel he was laid ; and the Cross of Hym who was our Example and Exemplar.

"Braineton, he didde much, for he was Geomancer to ye Abbey of old tyme."

These curious statements appear to have a bearing on certain facts recorded of the Lady Chapel and upon others which have come to light as a result of the study of the whole plan of the Abbey Church and Monastic buildings. The latter were found to be laid out on a series of commensurate squares of 37 × 2 (or 74) feet, and it has been observed that there is no divergence from the symmetry of these squares in the works of the successive centuries right up to the time of the last Abbot, for the Edgar Chapel falls into line

[1] William of Malmesbury's *Glastonbury*, quoted below.

with the rest.   Thus the outer measure of the total length of the Great Church with St. Mary's Chapel is 592 feet, or eight commensurate and consecutive squares of 74 feet each, and the width of the Nave and Quire are each one such square.   The plan has been already most useful in locating the position of walls destroyed and lost.   There is much yet to be done in order to complete the plan, but it is, in the main, recovered, and has been published in the *Proceedings of the Somerset Archæological Society*, from which it is here reproduced (Fig. 12).

As to the engraved geometric lines on the floor of St. Mary's Chapel, it may be well to quote William of Malmesbury, whose record of this dates from the twelfth century.   This old chronicler says, speaking of this chapel, which was on the site of the oldest Christian church:

"This church, then, is certainly the oldest I know in England, and from this circumstance derives its name (*vetusta ecclesia*). . . . In the pavement may be seen on every side stones designedly inlaid in triangles and squares, and figured with lead, under which, if I believe some sacred enigma to be contained, I do no injustice to religion."

The plan of the Chapel is itself a perfect instance of the Vesica Piscis, the proportions of the double equilateral triangle and the most sacred and cherished mystery of the Christian temple builders (see *Proceedings of the Somerset Archæological Society*, vol. lxii., 1916, pp. xxxviii-xl).

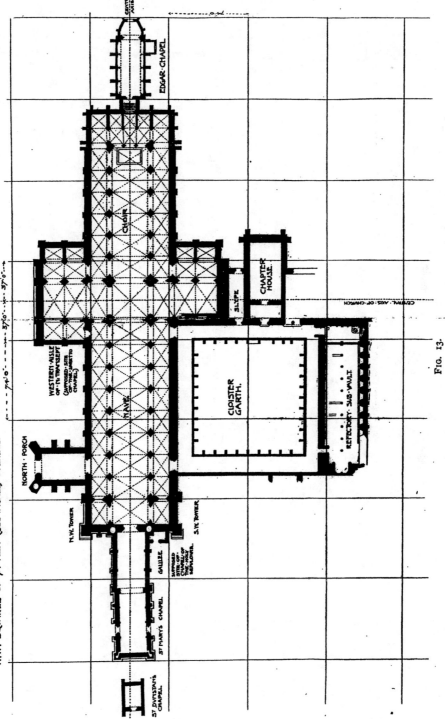

GLASTONBURY · ABBEY

GENERAL · PLAN · CORRECTED · TO · DATE · (1912)
WITH · SQUARES · OF · 74 · FEET (888 INCHES) OVERLAID.

CENTRAL · AXIS

EDGAR · CHAPEL

Choir

CHAPTER
HOUSE

SLYPE

WESTERN · AISLE
OF · TH · TRANSEPT
(SUPPOSED · SITE
OF · THE · LORETTO
CHAPEL)

NAVE

CLOISTER
GARTH.

CENTRAL · AXIS · OF · CHURCH

NORTH · PORCH

N.W. TOWER

REFECTORY · SUB · VAULT

S.W. TOWER

GALILEE

SUPPOSED
SITE · OF
CHAPEL · OF
THE · HOLY
SEPULCHRE.

ST MARY'S · CHAPEL

ST DUNSTAN'S
CHAPEL

FIG. 13.

NOTE.—This plan shows the state of knowledge in 1912. A western aisle to the north transept is shown on the site of
the foundations which had been discovered.

To fold between pp. 148, 149.

For the " Four Ways " see such early instances of the Rood as the example at Lucca Cathedral, where the arms of the Cross are held in a circle, suggestive of the zodiac, and point to the position of the four fixed signs Aquarius, Leo, Taurus, and Aquila or Scorpio, corresponding to SS. Matthew, Mark, Luke, and John, figured in the Christian symbology by the Angel, the Lion, the Bull, and the Eagle respectively. What is implied in the foregoing communication, when it is stated that of the four ways, they only builded two, is not known to the writer.

F.B.B., not being yet quite satisfied on the subject of the script of 13th June, 1911, repeated a part of his former question, as follows:

Q. " But where was that building 22 feet long and 4 paces wide, with three four-light windows and fans. I cannot see how the measure of 22 feet is obtained. Was this an east-and-west measure, or to be taken north-and-south ?"

A. " Ye door into ye transept in ye north, which I, Camel, used ; he was in ye west porche and under the three high windowes.

" What wold ye ? The newe Chappell, he was in ye Bank far oute, in line with ye Transept as I remember yt. He wasne finished or ever. Chappells a many ! Everywhere ! Why cumbered they the ground when faith was dead, and there was no longer any need for hym ? The purse[1] was full, it must be spent, and so, when nor barn nor byre nor pent called for it, it was yspent. Why should roysterers and evil men have it to spend ? So we builded much.

" Chapels everywhere—ne need of them.

" Small chance it is preserved (*passage doubtful*), but it was well ycovered, I wot, for them who would pull downe.

---

[1] John Camel was " Purse-bearer " to Abbot Bere.

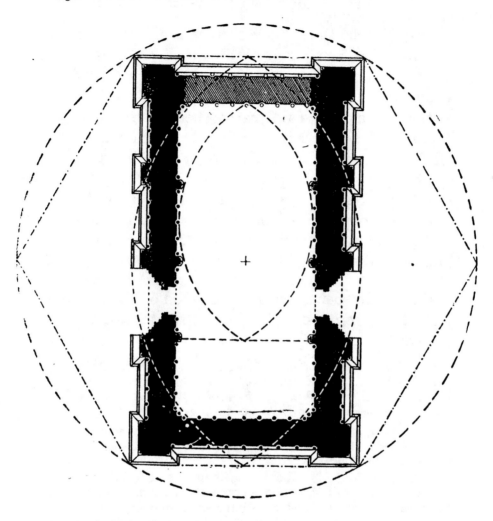

INDICATE EXISTING WALLS
                    FORMER EAST WALL.

FIG. 14.—GLASTONBURY ABBEY: PLAN OF THE CHAPEL OF
    OUR LADY, BUILT A.D. 1184, ON THE SITE OF THE CHURCH
    OF JOSEPH OF ARIMATHÆA.

The plan lies in a hexagon. Its measures are based upon the
    standard British foot of 12 inches. The breadth between the
    faces of the central buttresses is 37 feet, in harmony with the
    general scheme of measures found in the Abbey. The length
    of the vesica is approximately 64 feet, and its points touch

"Stones carven and yguilded—ne spirit, I wot. How could these things stand in the day of wrath? Pride! Ostentation! Much glory and much tinsel; but ne worship, ne humbleness, ne object for us to continue more. . . . So passe old tymes away."

Q. "But how was that 22 feet length arrived at?"

A. "A cloyster from ye Nave to ye Lobby, and four steppes unto ye Transept floor, and from ye lobby, on ye west, ye Chappell.

"Ne Chappell but ye Cloyster in ye corner of ye grete Church. Claustrum to ye Chappel along ye aisle—then ye lobby and ye Chappel west of hym."

This statement is now sufficiently explicit. It is possible to form a plan (see Figs. 15 and 16). The little cloister alongside the wall of the transept forms a western aisle to the same, covering one bay, whose width is known to have been 22 feet nearly. At this point it merges into a lobby or vestibule, at or near the foot of a fair-sized turret which stands at the north-west angle of the transept. This lobby has doors on all sides—(1) south, from the cloister communicating with the nave; (2) north, to the upper garth, and the

---

the outer faces of the end walls. External to this is another vesica embracing the plinth-course (see plan). The interior shows a third, marking three-quarters of its length. Each vesica contains a rhombus of two equilateral triangles. Their measures are symbolic and explanatory of the sacred geometry of which the " Gematria " of the Greek scriptures is illustrative. Thus, the solid rectangular area of this building is 37 by 64, or 2,368 square feet, by Gematria the equivalent of ΙΗΣΟΥΣ ΧΡΙΣΤΟΣ (Jesus Christ) or Ὁ ΑΓΙΟΣ ΤΩΝ ΑΓΙΩΝ (The Holy One of Holy Ones). The rhombus contained has the area 1,184 square feet, very possibly designed to record the date (A.D. 1184) of the erection of the Chapel. It will be noted that William of Malmesbury alludes to the " sacred enigma " believed to be concealed in the triangular and other figures on the floor of the Chapel.

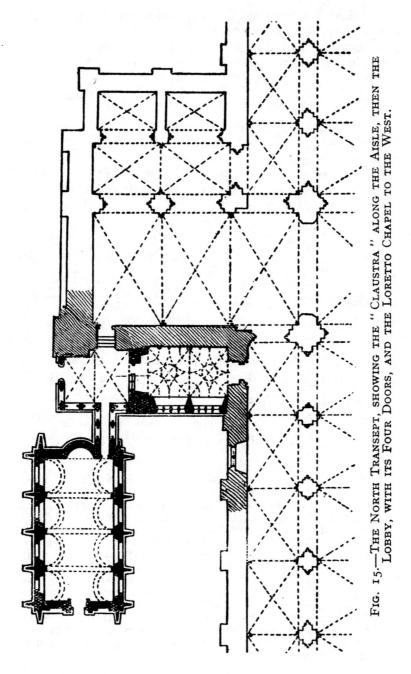

FIG. 15.—THE NORTH TRANSEPT, SHOWING THE "CLAUSTRA" ALONG THE AISLE, THEN THE LOBBY, WITH ITS FOUR DOORS, AND THE LORETTO CHAPEL TO THE WEST.

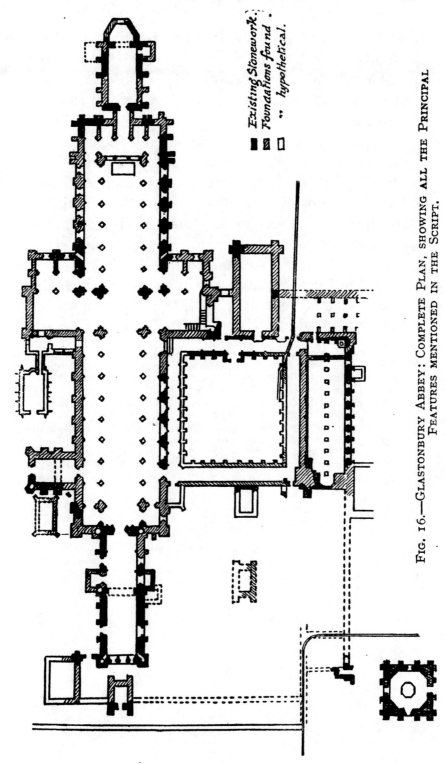

Fig. 16.—Glastonbury Abbey: Complete Plan, showing all the Principal Features mentioned in the Script.

path used by Camel the Purser, who lived in High Street; (3) east, and up the steps through the transept wall, into the transept itself; and (4) west, into the short corridor of 10 feet leading to the Loretto Chapel.

A final question was asked, and the result is interesting, as the question was a mental one, asked by F.B.B., not written nor communicated to J.A. by any ostensible means. F.B.B. formulated the question in his mind thus: " What was the surname of the Paduan architect Francesco?" Answer: " *Vecchi.—Francesco di Vecchi.*"[1]

This not being quite as clear as was wished, the question was repeated, and the reply came as follows: " VECCHI *di Torcello in Italia.*"

[1] A name unknown to us in this connection.—F.B.B. A letter received by F.B.B. from an Englishman living in Venice (dated April 19) gives the following extract from the " Curiosita Veneziane " (Giuseppe Tassini, Venezia, 1887) :

" *Vecchia* . . . Stefano della Vecchia. Il cui padre Venturino era stato approvato cittadino originario il 29 Octobre 1629 apparteneva alla famiglia Della Vecchia, la quali venne dal territorio di Bergamo, ed era detto da principio, Cornovi.

" . . . Un Antonio di questa famiglia il cui figlio Zaccaria fu *Vescovo di Torcello,* comperi in 1565 un nobile palazzo sulla Fundamenta della Madonna dell'Orto."

PLATE V.

CONJECTURAL RECONSTRUCTION OF THE NORTH TRANSEPT, WITH
THE "CLAUSTRUM" ATTACHED.

On the left, under the turret, is the open vestibule, leading to the Chapel
of the Loretto (on extreme left).

To face page 154.

CONCLUSION

So ends the "Loretto Chapel" script, with a
series of precise and categorical statements, offer-
ing no means of escape from the final alternative
of truth or falsehood, fact or fiction. This situa-
tion will be clear to the reader, as it is to the writer
of this narrative, who, for the reasons now about
to be given, entertains no misgivings as to the
course he has taken in publishing it.

His motto here would be, " Prove all things,
and hold fast that which is good." These writings,
whose value is at present unproven, and in respect
of the detailed statement of names, dates, and
places, highly problematical, are put forward as
an illustration of the working of his method.

They are not to be accepted with credulity,
but are subjects for critical analysis, and must be
weighed and examined, with all the rest, in the
light of reason, assisted by every useful means of
normal research and exploration.

If we are resolved to accept nothing which is not
first fully endorsed by reason and common sense,
and afterwards fortified by deductions fairly made
from data, however slender, we stand but little
risk of being deceived. Let us, therefore, apply
to this case the same rule which the writer has

already successfully applied in the case of the
Edgar Chapel.

Intuition has played her part. From the depths
of the subconscious mind her power has evoked
these images. Now let Reason and Logic take
the reins and drive the argument. Let us analyse
the facts, such as they are, which bear upon the
case, and in the light of the intuitive results see
whether an argument may be built up which will
be capable of supporting weight.

In this lies the true utility of the method we
have chosen. It claims a double value—(1) in
its ability to remember and to review subcon-
sciously an infinitude of minor things, slightly or
casually impressed upon the mind and unnoticed
or unremembered by the working brain; and (2)
the faculty of balancing, assessing, and combining
these in such manner as the brain itself is rarely
if ever able to do, and hence to evolve from slenderest data a scheme in which all probabilities
which can lawfully be inferred from these minutiæ
are welded into a complete whole.

For a moment, let us go farther and assume
that some of the statements made in the script
are not merely incapable of proof, but are found
actually inconsistent with facts. Where then do
we stand with our theory ?

As I have said, until the statements are accepted,
no one is deceived unless by his own rashness.
All that has happened is that two people having a
perfectly honest purpose have attempted to record
by automatic process knowledge arrived at by the

trained exercise of the subconscious mind, and have obtained—let us say—fiction or romance instead of the fact they sought.

The logical inference from this failure will obviously be that the particular method employed, whilst it may have the value claimed for it of supplementing the ordinary reasoning powers, has proved unreliable where applied for the purpose of procuring statements whose truth does not (as in the case of the Edgar Chapel) depend upon the deductive or inductive probabilities, but upon isolated facts unrelated to others, such as the names of places and people unknown; and that therefore, as a general conclusion, the method is unsuited for the purpose of obtaining such information, and we have used it for an end for which it is not adapted.

Thus may the legitimate bounds of the automatic method be prescribed; Intuition must bring all her results to the bar of Reason for provisional acceptance, and when this test is passed then the matter becomes ripe for further research.

Above all, let us not be superstitious. There is no need to invoke the action of supernatural agencies of a malevolent sort to explain the outcome of our own fallibility. If a man or woman sits down and produces automatically a story which turns out to be fiction, why, I ask, should that fiction be regarded as anything inherently worse in origin than the mass of fiction, good, bad, and indifferent, which writers produce consciously?

Where is the essential difference? The only

answer I can find to this question is that the
difference lies in the folly of the credulous, who
are at all times willing to attach greater importance and credit to a statement made from an unknown source than to one which has a definite
human and personal origin. " Omne ignotum
pro magnifico."

For the imaginative function, whether working
consciously or unconsciously, is the same in either
case. Give it truth to feed upon and it will
evolve truth. And through the door of truth
may enter that which will guide us to a wider
knowledge.

Δ

APPENDIX

THE LORETTO CHAPEL

SYNTHETIC OR CONSTRUCTIVE ARGUMENT

BASED ON CONCLUSIONS OFFERED BY THE AUTOMATIC SCRIPT, AND THE WEIGHING OF ALL AVAILABLE DATA IN THE LIGHT OF SAME.

A.—AS TO THE POSITION OF THE LORETTO CHAPEL.

SCRIPT.

August 16, 1917. "Deepe, by ye Bank, is ye walle," etc. "But capella wasne in muro in Boreali parte . . . and in ye Banke deepe downe ye shall find him," etc. There was a deep place where they destroyed, and they covered him, and made a banke full six feet high, and soe saved the wall at the west end for all tyme."

EXISTING DATA.

The Deep Place.—The mention of a "deep place" calls attention for the first time to a number of facts which group themselves in a manner suggestive of such a probability. They are as follows:

(*a*) Stukeley's view (1723) (see Fig. 9) seems to indicate a drop on the north side of the nave and transept, to a lower level.

Coney's view (see Plate IV.) certainly shows the small building on the north side of the nave with a break in the ground just in front of it, marking a lower level for the wall.

(*b*) The configuration of the ground is in favour of this. Above and eastward of the Abbey enclosure is a narrow valley running west, and filled

WORKING HYPOTHESIS.

That the ground on the north side of the Church sloped down formerly to the bed of the brook coming from the hill behind the town. This would make a depression about 10 feet deep alongside the Church, at a distance, roughly, of about 40 feet north of the outer face of the nave aisle wall, and immediately north of the projection of the north transept and porch. The bed would have been partly filled when the Abbey was standing, and there would be a system of drains beneath the soil, which would have been levelled to form a garth or garden a few feet below the nave floor, terminated on the west by a

December 4, 1916. " Abbot Bere ybuilded ye Loretto Chapel faire and large to the north side of the Navis. Itt was not ye Chapitre House. . . . Bere's Chapel was distant from ye Navis thirty-one feet and a half, and from ye aisle of ye transept he was fulle tenn feet. . . The same was forty feet by twenty or thereabouts, and his chief doore was to the west, and a pavement joyned him to the road from St. John's Gate to ye Churche."

August 17, 1917. " Capella Loretta was on ye lower level, with four or six steppys up to the pavement."

" Seek my chapple, as I told ye, in ye Banck."

up in its lower part, over which lies the northern section of the Abbey enclosure. The High Street runs down the north side of this valley, and parallel to it, and closely adjoining the Abbey wall is Silver Street, a name said by some antiquaries to indicate a ford.

(c) The drainage of the Abbey church is down the north side, as would appear by the direction of the drainage channel in the foundations of the Edgar Chapel, and the larger water-channel whose course was traced diagonally beneath the floor of the quire.

(d) In excavating the north porch, a very deep pit was found right against the north-west angle of the footings. It went down nearly 10 feet below the floor-level of the church. This may have extended east and west, and the north porch may in that case be supposed to have been approached by a paved way over a bridge.

The Bank.—The foot of the bank, as nearly as may be estimated, lies about 27 feet north of the position of the nave wall (outer face). This would bring the 31 and a half feet distance indicated by the script for the wall of the chapel, about 4 and a half feet within the

path or pavement from the porch to St. John's Gate (running due north), and beyond this, again to the west, would be another garth at a still lower level, to the north of St. Mary's Chapel and the Galilee, following the general trend of the grounds, which slope to the westward. This part was the cemetery of the laity.

It is inferred that Bere's Chapel of the Loretto may have stood on the upper garth, its floor a few feet below the nave, and at about the distance mentioned in the script.

That the present aspect of the ground, which shows a uniform rise to the north of the Abbey, is thus totally misleading, and the bank and the higher level beyond on the town side must be altogether artificial, and nothing but

11

SYNTHETIC OR CONSTRUCTIVE ARGUMENT—*Continued.*

SCRIPT.

"He was entered from ye west, and had a door into the littel cloister by ye transept of ye grete Church, and four stepps up to the pavement."

"All ye measures were marked plaine on ye slabbes of St. Mary's Chappel . . . so it was recorded, as they who builded and they who came after knew aforehand where they should build."

"The newe chappell he was in ye bank far oute in line with ye transept as I remember it."

September 1, 1910. "On ye north syde of ye grete church, at ye ende, near to ye newe chappel which Bere (builded)."

EXISTING DATA.

bank, and this would seem to accord with the old gardener's recollection.

The bank runs westwards as far as the north porch, or about 108 feet west of the transept, so that the west end of the chapel as described would be well covered, being some 40 feet east of the termination of the bank.

The extreme projection of the transept, beyond the line of the inner face of the nave wall, would be about 60 feet, and not less than 54.

The thirty-one and a half feet measure from the outside of the nave wall, if added to the probable thickness of the latter, will give a total of 39 or 40 feet, and if this measure is assumed to be to the inner face of the chapel wall (south) the position of its outer face would accord with the 37 feet general line, following the symmetric scheme on which the whole abbey is found to be built (see Fig. 12), and the north side of the chapel will then come very nearly into line with the transept.

WORKING HYPOTHESIS.

a huge accumulation of débris from the destruction of the Abbey. The bulk of the ancient work now destroyed was so enormous that there is no difficulty at all in supposing this, notwithstanding the fact that a great quantity of the masonry went, as is known, to make a foundation for the new road to Wells.

The further inference is made that under this bank will most likely be hidden a great deal of fragmentary work, and that its removal will bring to light many things of archæological interest.

That the Loretto Chapel, if its position be correctly given in the script as 31 feet 6 inches from nave, would appear nearly in line with the transept (north end), when viewed from the north, but, if anything, rather further out (see Fig. 14).

B.—As to the Western Aisle to the Transept, and the Suggestion of a Cloister or Passage in Same, and the Character of the Building.

June 13, 1911. . . . "Somewhat remaineth of ye outer walls, and ye walle by ye crossinge. . . . Ye doore unto hym is at the west (see note), nigh unto the pillar of the Navis; one doore only, on Nave.

"Yn feete twenty and two, and foure paces in the width thereof, and ye walle of ye Nave was strengthened thereby," etc.

December 4, 1916. "Bere's Chapel was distant from ye Navis thirty-one feet and a half, and from *ye aisle of ye transept* he was fulle tenn feet with a covered way unto, and four steppes up unto *ye aisle* aforesaid.

"There were four steppes—nay, six—to the *aisle of ye transept*, and a covered way vaulted in a round vault to ye chappel."

August 17, 1917. "Claustra quae vocantur, vento Boreale aperta est—in vestibule sub turre—English volts."

(Italics mine.—F.B.B.)

(*a*) The wall-footing discovered in 1911 shows a possible breadth of 12 feet or so for this aisle. The thickness of the footing is evidence of a strong construction. There were some marks of a cross-foundation at a point over 20 feet out north, and near the face of the bank.

(*b*) The indications were in favour of a lower level for this work. The drop from the transept level to that of the nave is about 4 feet, and this aisle or passage would appear to be on the nave level.

(*c*) Benedictine houses did not usually have western aisles to the transepts, as is the case with cathedral churches. But Glastonbury followed Wells in some things, and at Wells there are western aisles to the transepts, and that on the north side has screens on two sides, within arches to nave and to transept.

(*d*) The detail found on this site was of very fine late perpendicular window-tracery, showing the existence of windows with heavy central mullions, and most likely of four lights.

That the foundation discovered in 1911 *is not that of a chapel, nor yet of an aisle to the transept, properly so called, although it might be thus described since it would have that appearance from without.*

The inference is that this adjunct would have been on the nave level, and its use connected with the nave. It would have been primarily a passage-way from the nave to a court or to buildings on the north side, and it would be properly described as a cloister alley.

In this position it would, if substantially built, most readily serve the useful purpose of contributing support to the central tower and to the walls near the crossing, adding stability to the transept if affected by the weakness of the tower, and furnishing support for flying buttresses to the north-west angle of the crossing and tower itself.

There would be little object in

SYNTHETIC OR CONSTRUCTIVE ARGUMENT—*Continued.*

SCRIPT.	EXISTING DATA.	WORKING HYPOTHESIS.
"Seek my chapple as I told ye in ye Banck. He was entered from ye west, and had a door into the *littel cloister by ye transept* of ye grete church, and four stepps up to the pavement. Ye door was in ye transept wall at ye end thereof." "Ye door into ye transept in ye north, which I, Camel, used, he was in ye west porche and under the three high windows. "*A Cloyster from ye Nave to ye Lobby*, and four steppes unto ye Transept floor, and from ye Lobby, on ye west, ye Chappell. "*Ne Chappel but ye Cloyster* in ye corner of ye grete church. *Claustrum ta ye Chappel along ye aisle, then ye lobby* and ye Chappel west of hym." (Italics mine.—F.B.B.)	(e) Camel's house was in the High Street at a point which would be readily approached by a path towards this part of the Abbey Church.	carrying it out further north than would be requisite to cover one bay of the transept wall. This would make it a possible 22 feet in internal measure. There would be normally a double square on plan, and if fan-vaulted this would give two bays, and two windows to the west and one to the north—three in all.

C.—AS TO THE ITALIAN STYLE OF THE CHAPEL.

December 4, 1916. "**Abbot Bere ybuilded ye Loretto Chapel faire and large, to the north** (side	(a) The Chapel was built just after Bere's embassage to Italy. He was a cultivated and learned man with a	*That a Chapel dedicated to an "Italian" Madonna, erected by an Abbot of liberal views, im-*

pressed by the newer learning and culture, immediately on his return from a visit to Italy, at a time when the forms of Italian Renaissance were in process of adaptation to Gothic buildings, might well have been influenced in its design by Italian ideas, even to a wholesale extent, and that if an Italian master were employed, as appears by no means an unreasonable idea, an entirely Italian model may have been followed.

knowledge of architecture, as is evident from the quality of his building works. He must have been supported by capable, if not eminent, master-builders and craftsmen.

(b) Bere was impregnated with the new ideas, and was the friend of Erasmus. A letter of his to Erasmus is extant. His sympathy with new and more liberal views would be reflected in a wider culture, and the influence of the Italian Renaissance, already affecting English art in minor ways, may well have moved him to become a pioneer in introducing the style which, a half-century later, usurped the place of our native "Tudor" forms. These he used as a master, and had developed them to their highest pitch.

(c) The duration of his visit to Italy is at present unknown to us, but the circumstance of the death of Pius III.—if he overstayed that event—would make for delay and give him time to devote to the study of Italian architectural models.

(d) The circumstances of his vow are also, so far as we know, not a matter of history; but the vow itself or the intention which clearly implies it is our reading of Leland's note.

of the) Navis.... Yt was ybuilded by Bere most faire and wonderful in ye newe style brought from Ytaly when he didd go there...."

"We have said, he was of the Ytalian style, new and very faire, and Bere ybuilded coming from embassadrie in Ytaly.... He wasne like anything else, (but was of the) newe style."

Here followed the detailed sketches showing—

1. A rectangular chapel of four bays, with a small apse to the east, as a "Cava Virginis."

2. Parapets of undulating outline, and others suggestive of the fleur-de-lys, with indications of fruit and flower enrichment.

3. Sitting lions, bearing shields, over each division of the bays, mounted on small pillars with "patellae" or plaques, dividing the parapets.

4. Heads of angels or cherubs, probably in the cornices.

5. Round-headed windows, and vaults with bands of carved fruit and flowers on the groin-ribs.

SYNTHETIC OR CONSTRUCTIVE ARGUMENT—*Continued.*

SCRIPT.

August 16, 1917. "**Maestro Francesco de Padua qui me instruxit et capellam cognoscit in Italia . . . struebat in modo Italiano.**

"**Francesco de Padua aedificavit. Two would speak of it—he who made it, and I who moved for my fannes and English. We both made him.**"

(*Name of the model for this work*)—

"**Capella di Marco at Padua—hym by the Key.**"

"**Domenic di Vallera Castiglione aedificavit anno 1497—via St. Ursula.**"

(*Name of Bere's architect*)—"**Vecchi—Francesco De Vecchi.**"

"**VECCHI di Torcello in Italia.**"

EXISTING DATA.

The Chapel is undoubtedly a thank-offering. It is built to the honour of Our Lady in the particular aspect of an "Italian" saint of local repute, possessed of the attribute of protection to life and health. The choice of a style and character for the monument designed by Bere would very naturally be consonant with that prevailing locally —*i.e.*, Italian.

(*e*) A few fragments of plain moulded work, of Italian character, have been noted amongst the débris of the Abbey. These were hitherto supposed to have belonged to some Elizabethan building, now destroyed, whose remains had somehow found their way into the general mass of Abbey fragments.

WORKING HYPOTHESIS.

That the type that would evoke most readily the Abbot's artistic sympathies would be a North Italian type, not too far removed from the principles of architectural form to which he had been habituated. An entirely Roman model, on purely classic lines, is for this reason less likely. But the selection of an Italian master for the purpose of carrying out Bere's scheme almost necessarily follows if the intention to employ an Italian style be conceded. Bere could not do this unaided, as an Abbot would not be his own architect.

D.—As to the Style of the Building at the Angle of the Transept and North Aisle of Nave.

Script, June 13, 1911. "I made that building. All that I didde anywhere is fannes. Ne barrel vault. And under them, three faire windowes of foure lights, with transomes and littel castel-work on the ramps thereof ... and each fanne had of ... and they were twelve ribs, and they were ycoloured red and gold, like my chapel of Edgar. ...

"... Ye roundels of ye volte were golden, and also ye bosses, and ye hollows were bright redde. likewise ye tabernacle of Oure Ladye in the est wall golde and redde; and ye windowes were of glasse yellow in canopies with redde and blewe in ye little lights thereof. Ye floore was of tileis red, with shields and ornaments in yellow likewise." ...

(a) As an integral part of the Church the probabilities lie in the direction of the use of Bere's own master-masons for this work, and the choice of the customary English style seems to follow. This would be all the more consistent with probabilities if the work were involved with the strengthening of the older masonry at the crossing of the Church—a work known to have been necessary, since Leland records the fact that Bere strengthened the central tower by the addition of the "St. Andrew's" arches beneath it (see Plate III).

(b) The fragments of window-tracery already referred to as having been found on the site are English in character.

That the building in the angle of the nave and transept was formed with the double object of a support to the weak walls of the crossing, and as a covered approach to the Chapel of the Loretto, erected by Abbot Bere on a site adjoining the north side of the nave, but not attached directly to same, and that this cloister was built in the later English style in which his own masons were expert.

ENVOI

THE LAMPLIGHTER

ONE by one, along the crowded street
The footsteps falter, and the stillness grows
Oppressive as the sudden hush that falls
In shaded chambers whence a life has flown.
One by one, the ruddy windows fade
To utter darkness, while behind closed doors
The voices cease, and all the shadowy night
Broods o'er a city of the seeming dead;
Save only that amid the shadows gleam
Dim lights that trace the form of street and square
And guide the wanderer in his mazy quest
Through ways all unfamiliar.   He that lit
The starry welcome now is seen no more.
His light extinguished and his duty done,
He peaceful sleeps within his silent home.
We see him not; and yet perchance he hears
In dreams our echoing voices as we pass
Athwart his shuttered windows—hears us bless
The light he lighted, gleaming through the night
A welcome to the lost and weary; wakes perchance
To murmur, " All is well," then sleeps again.
So may he sleep in peace until the Sun
From which his flame was borrowed wakes the East
To crimson glory, and his glimmering lights
Merge in the splendour of the breaking Day.

JOHN ALLEYNE.

INDEX AND SYNOPSIS

169

BILLING AND SONS, LTD., PRINTERS, GUILDFORD, ENGLAND